"This is a most uplifting book for those who are facing deep waters. As someone living with a terminal and incurable disease, I find the stories in this book to be profoundly encouraging."

—DR. ED DOBSON, *senior pastor,*
Calvary Church, Grand Rapids, Michigan

"In these difficult days, this is a must-read for all who feel their faith slipping. Dr. Tony Beckett's thesis, 'God is good,' needs to be affirmed again and again. But it isn't enough to just say the words; the truth of it must be put into practice. *God Is Good* will assist the reader in doing just that. I commend it highly."

—DR. DONALD R. HUBBARD, *former pastor of*
Calvary Baptist Church, New York City; itinerant Bible teacher

TONY BECKETT

DISCOVERING

HIS FAITHFULNESS IN

FAITHLESS TIMES

NAVPRESS

Bringing Truth to Life
P.O. Box 35001, Colorado Springs, Colorado 80935

The Navigators is an international Christian organization. Our mission is to reach, disciple, and equip people to know Christ and to make Him known through successive generations. We envision multitudes of diverse people in the United States and every other nation who have a passionate love for Christ, live a lifestyle of sharing Christ's love, and multiply spiritual laborers among those without Christ.

NavPress is the publishing ministry of The Navigators. NavPress publications help believers learn biblical truth and apply what they learn to their lives and ministries. Our mission is to stimulate spiritual formation among our readers.

ISBN 1-57683-340-2

Cover design: Dan Jamison
Cover illustration: Andrew Judd/Masterfile
Creative Team: Nanci McAlister, Brad Lewis, Nat Akin, Laura Spray, Glynese Northam

Some of the anecdotal illustrations in this book are true to life and are included with the permission of the persons involved. All other illustrations are composites of real situations, and any resemblance to people living or dead is coincidental.

Beckett, Tony.
  God is good : discovering his faithfulness in faithless times / Tony Beckett.
      p. cm.
Includes bibliographical references.
  ISBN 1-57683-340-2
  1. Christian life. 2. God--Goodness. I. Title.
  BV4501.3 .B43 2002
  248.8'6--dc21
                                    2002008417

Printed in the United States of America
1 2 3 4 5 6 7 8 9 10 / 06 05 04 03 02

DEDICATION

To the men of
The Church Behind the Wall
S.C.I. Dallas
Dallas, Pennsylvania

Tony Beckett
2 Cor 12:9

CONTENTS

ACKNOWLEDGMENTS

It was Carlton Houck's idea—actually it was his burden that reached out not only to prisoners at the penitentiary near his home but also to me, his pastor. He wanted me to go to prison, in the right sense. So I did, expecting one thing but experiencing quite another, because in this place my soul was moved by a simple answer/response: God is good. All the time.

For many years, Carlton and his wife, Pam, have ministered faithfully to the men at the State Correctional Institute in Dallas, Pennsylvania, going where some would fear to go, where some wouldn't take the time to go. It became my privilege to support, encourage, facilitate, and participate in teaching the Word to a group of men who have learned the grace of God and experienced change and forgiveness.

May their experiences help teach you that, indeed, God is good.

INTRODUCTION

Sometimes in the most unlikely of settings God takes the expected, reshapes it into the unexpected, and replaces our agenda with His curriculum. And maybe—just maybe—He reveals Himself in a new way, with a new perspective, and with a freshness that affects us from that moment forward.

"God is good," the man at the front of the church said. No warning, no introductory thoughts, no humor to warm up the crowd and capture their attention. Just a three-word sentence. This wasn't something that would raise the attention of the average attendee in some settings, but it was more than enough to get a rousing response that day. No one told me what would happen next, nor could anyone have fully prepared me for the impact that the next words would have.

The group of nearly two hundred men responded immediately, emphatically. As with one voice they answered, "All the time."

"All the time," replied the man at the front, echoing their response—a heartfelt affirmation of this truth. His sincere enthusiasm was evident as he repeated their words.

Present for the first time, I was unaware of this unscripted call to worship. They all knew the lines. I didn't. And what I really didn't realize was that God was putting my toes on the brink of stretching the comfortable confines of my soul, making room for a realization that His goodness is sometimes better recognized in prison than in my church.

"God is good, all the time."

When we got out of the car that night, my friend Carlton had said, "You can hear the brothers warming up for church!" Even outside the prison gates we could indeed hear the band. The guarded walls and wires couldn't keep the sound inside the State Correctional Institute in Dallas, Pennsylvania. "You might as well take everything that you don't need out of your pockets, especially gum," he said. So after putting my wallet, pocket change, and cough drops in the glove compartment, we locked the car and headed to the guardhouse.

You don't just walk into prison. First you do paperwork—a form filled out weeks in advance—a "clean check" sheet. Then you come to the door at the gatehouse, locked until a guard inside presses the buzzer and allows you to open the door. "Sign in here," he says, and pushes a clipboard toward you. Name, address, time in, purpose, and a space for time out.

The guard slid a small, flat wooden box across the counter and into it I placed my Bible, emptied what little was still in my pockets, then added my watch, glasses, and belt. Under the watchful eyes of two correction officers, I stepped slowly through a metal detector.

The guard gave each of us a visitor badge. Then, with our belts back into our pant loops and Bibles in hand, we were led out into an open area between fences topped with concertina, a razor-sharp form of barbed wire. We passed through another gate, then stood between two gates where a sign directed us to look toward the camera monitoring our progress. As one gate closed, we were held in that enclosure until the next gate opened and we stepped into the yard. The church sat off to our left.

The church. I learned that it wasn't just a chapel, but a church. Yes, it's a building provided by the state for religious purposes, and a variety of groups use it. But remember, the church isn't a building, but people. In this building, a unique congregation gathers, one that taught me invaluable lessons.

Their pastor is the Protestant prison chaplain, officially, but in reality, the pastor of "a church behind the wall." This is a dynamic, diverse, devoted, and discipling church that, in the pastor's words, is a church where "we don't shoot our wounded, every dollar is a mission dollar, and we hope to lose all our members."

"We don't shoot our wounded." One time, the nervousness of a member of our group was obvious. It is, after all, prison—not the minimum-security kind and definitely not the "country club" for white-collar criminals that some might imagine. The walls are block, the floor is bare cement, and the doors are heavy for security purposes. We constantly received instructions as to where to stand, what to do, and where to go. Everyone else is dressed in cocoa-brown prison uniforms with D.O.C.—Department of Corrections—printed on their pant legs.

One of the prisoners with us in the chaplain's office could sense the nervous edge, so he spoke up. "No need to be afraid, because you're in the safest place in this prison." There we sat in our middle-class whiteness, getting schooled by someone with far more street smarts than we had collectively.

"It's the safest place for two reasons," he said. What followed were words I want never to forget and words that I have often repeated.

"First, this is God's house.

"And second, the brothers have decided that there's not going to be any trouble in God's house."

End of discussion.

Those words sunk deeply and embedded themselves into my brain, because far too often the church has been a place of hurt—not a place of safety, but of trouble. Sometimes the church just isn't a safe place. We screen our prayer requests before we speak. We carefully test and develop our confidences. We're afraid to trust others because, perhaps some time ago, we shared a confidence that wasn't kept.

"The brothers have decided that there's not going to be any trouble in God's house."

That's the way it should be! Many times I've stood in pulpits and quoted that prisoner, that one who knew and spoke a truth that we need to hear.

"God is good."

"All the time."

"All the time."

"God is good."

The service was underway and soon it would be my turn to stand before the group—but I still didn't have a firm grip on the routine. So I stood, looked into the faces of men who had a faith in God, a belief in the goodness of God, a grasp of a holy truth—something they had to learn from the Word, not from their circumstances.

So now I will sometimes stand before a group and say, "I'm going to give you a brief test. Actually, it's a test to let me know something about you." Then I speak the words I learned in prison: "God is good." Sometimes the response is silence—they don't know the answer/response routine.

So I explain how it works, take them through it a time or two until they start to give me a strong response. Then comes the punch line.

"You know where I learned that? I learned it when I was in prison."

Of course, that doesn't make immediate sense.

But it should.

Because if you can't say it there, then you don't really know that:

"God is good."

"All the time."

Occasionally, I go back to the prison. My life is so different from that of prisoners, but in some ways it can be so similar. All of us can be imprisoned, perhaps not physically by bars but in a wide variety of other ways. It would be an honest statement to say that we all struggle at times, that we're all fellow prisoners who experience dark times that can incarcerate our souls.

The issue that needs to be resolved is this: In those times, can we say, "God is good"?

In Scripture, we find the help we need to break out of our

confinement. We find how to deal with the things that can imprison us—those times when we feel that the cell key has been turned and we're locked into depression, discouragement, and uncertainty.

You're going to read eight truths from Scripture offering evidence that, indeed, "God is good, all the time." These aren't a series of steps you take in succession. They're truths that you can let swarm and surround you. They're lessons you'll learn from real people in the Bible—some of whom were even prisoners themselves, all of whom knew the need to live the truth that "God is good."

So, let's go to prison together. No need to pass clean check, empty your pockets, sign in, or walk through a metal detector. Just open your Bible and allow some prisoners to teach you this truth:

God is good.

All the time.

WORSHIP WHEN IT HURTS — SING

ACTS 16

Give me two trees, Lord, just wide enough for a hammock
* between.*
Enough leaves to shade me from the sun and a gentle
* breeze would be nice.*
Keep the humidity low, the temperature comfortable.
There I will be able to say,
"This is the day the Lord has made; [I will] rejoice and be
* glad in it." (Psalm 118:24)*

I never claimed to be a poet, but my rudimentary attempt sort of makes you smile, doesn't it? It makes me look out the window and think about planting a couple of trees. I need something fast-growing so that someday at this house I can have a hammock — a symbol for me of the kind of enjoyable day when it's easy to say, "God is good all the time."

My wife's parents introduced me to the joy of hammocks. Strung low between two trees in their backyard was a white cord hammock, wide enough for two people. The next spring, for Father's Day, a hammock came to our house, not just for the day but for a lifetime in the backyard. A small rope tied to a nearby fence became the "motor." A slight pull on the rope and the hammock would rock ever so gently.

When we moved, I delighted that the backyard again had trees hammock-distance apart. That first spring I didn't wait for Father's Day, only for sunshine and some warmer temperatures. When you lie in a hammock, you experience no sense of confinement, just one of freedom and escape. In my eagerness to relax suspended above the ground between two trees, I'd sometimes wrap myself in an afghan to ward off cool temperatures. But in our next home, no hammock in the backyard; the trees were too young, too far apart. So, I thought about the fast-growing trees to hasten a return to hammock times, because when it's hammock time, it's easy to say, "This is the day the Lord has made; I will rejoice and be glad in it."

But what about the night when your car is the last one in the parking lot at the mall? And it's blizzardlike, with the snow blowing sideways. You open the hood because that's what everyone does when the car doesn't start. As you stare at the engine compartment, filled with motor, electronics, belts, and hoses, you already know the problem—you left on the lights. You even know the solution. But you don't own a set of jumper cables, no other cars are in sight, and your cell phone is on the kitchen table at home where you set it and forgot it before walking out the door.

What do you say then? Do you say, "This is the day the Lord has made; I will rejoice and be glad in it"? Probably not. If you did, they'd probably not only tow away your car, but take you away as well—to someplace where you can rest in peace and quiet. The dismal circumstances of the moment can entrap your attitude, imprison your emotions in a cell of despair.

When life is good, it's easy to say, "God is good." But it's a different story when life isn't so good. In the shuffle of events and emotions, we can lose the truth that God is good all the time. Instead, we tend to judge God's goodness based on what we're experiencing and start to think His goodness is limited. Maybe He just doesn't have enough to go around all the time. It's as if the music stopped and everyone sat down but you. No chair for you. The cakewalk goes on for everyone else, just not you.

We still *know* that God is good—we just lack the evidence. We start thinking about how we would like life to be, full of those "hammock times."

Sometimes it's easy to sing, sometimes not. Right now life might be good for you—you might even be in the hammock mode of life. But what about when the hammock is gone and life becomes a stranded-in-an-empty-parking-lot time? What about when no help is in sight, no tools on hand, no phone to use? There in the cold and darkness of a difficult time, the words could easily seem forced, not authentic, a repetition, a recital without meaning. If you say them out loud, you might even feel like you're mocking your life.

Yet the truth remains—God is good, all the time.

And you can say those words! While the things that imprison us vary, two men who were actually thrown in jail give us the first help for overcoming the dark times of life. Their names were Paul and Silas and their prison was in Philippi. Even though they were wrongly accused, physically abused, and incarcerated through a miscarriage of justice, when the night was darkest, they sang the loudest. They sang! From the dark depths of a dungeon, they turned their eyes to God, directed their hearts to Him in worship, and sang.

Prelude to a Dark Time

PAUL KNEW THAT difficulties are a part of ministry. On his first mission trip, he encountered satanic opposition, persecution, rejection, threats, and a stoning so severe that the attackers dragged his body outside the city, leaving it there thinking Paul was dead. He also experienced great successes, and—after much discussion— even an endorsement from the leadership of the church in Jerusalem. But even that didn't come without a fight! Some leaders disagreed about the ministries reaching out to Gentiles. Some thought they needed to make these nonJews more Jewish. Others, such as Paul and Barnabas, said no. There was sharp dispute and debate before James made a decision to move forward and support Paul (see Acts 15).

Conflict with others can put us in a cell; unresolved conflict locks the door. We don't need to be literally arrested, chained, and tormented by false accusations to feel the darkness of an emotional dungeon.

Paul's second trip began with an even more unexpected difficulty. This time, he didn't have a disagreement with people opposed to his message, but with someone who'd been his mentor and friend since the beginning of his life as a follower of Christ— Barnabas. As a result, they went their separate ways: Barnabas took John Mark and headed to Cyprus, while Paul teamed up with Silas and went back to Asia Minor. Undoubtedly, Paul at times would say to his new teammate, "When Barnabas and I were here before . . . " And perhaps his heart ached as he said it. But still he pressed on, knowing God had work for them to do. The ongoing challenges brought on by those disagreements weighed heavily on Paul—just as similarly trying times press on us.

Then the door closed, not by the hand of man but by the Spirit of God. The Holy Spirit kept them from preaching, kept them from entering new territory, kept them from their plans for ministry— kept them until God gave them a fresh vision. He kept them from going one direction so He could send them a different way—to a difficult place of His choosing.

Change can feel like an open door to a dungeon. We don't want to go that way, do that thing, experience that situation. It was as if the walls were being built around Paul and Silas—controversy, disagreement, change—walls that could have emotionally fenced them in.

A Powerful Ministry

IT WAS TIME to move across the sea to new territory. Late one night a man from Macedonia appeared to Paul in a vision, asking him to come and help. So, plans changed. No longer intent on revisiting past places of ministry or exploring new opportunities to preach in Asia, Paul and those with him immediately headed to Macedonia. They believed that the vision was from God. It was His will that they go there.

What could be better than that? They were where God wanted them to be, doing what God wanted them to do, in the way God wanted them to do it, at the time God wanted it done. Smack in the middle of God's will would seem like the place of greatest blessing, but calm can come before a storm and peacefulness occurs even in the middle of a hurricane. They went, unaware of the events that would soon unfold.

God launched Paul and Silas across the Aegean Sea, onto the continent of Europe and to the land of Macedonia. It would be a time of powerful ministry. They were exactly where God wanted them to be. His hand of blessing was upon them and He was changing their lives.

A Divine Appointment

First the travelers met Lydia, a first-century businesswoman who specialized in selling purple cloth. The Bible doesn't say whether she'd relocated to Philippi or was there on business from her hometown of Thyatira. But what is clear is that God set this divine appointment, one that brought the bearer of good news to a worshiper of the true God.

It was the Sabbath. Paul, Silas, and those traveling with them went to the river, expecting to find a place of prayer. Perhaps they didn't think they'd find a gathering of women there. Paul began to speak to these women—one of whom was Lydia—and God changed her life that day. He opened her heart and she responded to Paul's message. After being baptized, Lydia persuaded these itinerant ministers to stay at her house. When ministry is going well like this, it's easy to say, "God is good."

A Demon-Possessed Girl

Paul and his party next encountered an unnamed slave girl. She had a gift, some would say. But it was actually a demonic spirit that enabled her to tell the future. It was a "python" spirit, a mythical snake worshiped by those who came to the temple of Delphi. She became a source of income for her owners, men who were nothing more than spiritual pimps who sold her "services" for their profit. She could speak the truth, and she did: "These men are servants of the Most High God, who are telling you the way to be saved," she cried (Acts 16:17).

Not only does the message matter, but so does the messenger. Local people knew the reputation of this slave girl and her owners. They knew about the spirit within her, and now that demon was promoting Paul and Silas. The words she said were true, but they did more harm than good. It gave the impression that the two strangers were with her, were like her, and that they had a message that came to them as did hers. This had to stop.

By the power of God, Paul brought her shouting to a sudden conclusion. "In the name of Jesus Christ I command you to come out of her!" he said (16:18). Immediately, the spirit left. It was instantaneous and the change was obvious. No longer tormented, no longer crying out a message from the spirit, no longer a fortune-teller, she now was the recipient of God's power working in her life. A powerful ministry, evidenced in yet another changed life. A trip that began with delay and discouragement was now demonstrating the power of God. Paul and Silas must have felt great enthusiasm and encouragement as their ministry was changing lives. God is good, all the time!

It was a hammock time. God was blessing in obvious ways. They were experiencing the heady excitement of travel, the encouraging sense of God's presence, and the evidence of His blessing. Gone were the feelings of discouragement that had hung over the beginning of the trip like the low, looming clouds of a cold and blustery winter rain. Gone was the confusion, the bewilderment about why God was keeping them from ministry and closing the doors of opportunity. As they remained faithful, God swept the paths before them and made the way clear. Ministry was good.

A Prison Cell

ODDLY, THOUGH, THIS powerful ministry led them to a prison cell. You see, money can make people mad—especially losing money.

> *When the owners of the slave girl realized that their hope of*
> *making money was gone, they seized Paul and Silas and*
> *dragged them into the marketplace to face the authorities.*
> *They brought them before the magistrates and said, "These*
> *men are Jews, and are throwing our city into an uproar by*
> *advocating customs unlawful for us Romans to accept or*
> *practice." (Acts 16:19-20)*

These men had been making money off this girl and they weren't
happy that she was free from the spirit that possessed her. They
were mad and someone was going to pay, one way or another. So
they went after Paul and Silas.

Their accusation before the magistrates began with a racist
innuendo: "These men are Jews," they said. What did this statement add to their case against Paul and Silas? It simply intensified
the feelings of the crowd by pointing out the difference of their eth-
nicity. Even today, it's easy for race to enter a conversation, almost
unnoticed. A person tells an incident or story to another, mention-
ing the race of someone involved. The fact is included only to point
out that particular difference. Sometimes subtly, often times obviously, usually, it's not mentioned unless there's a difference. That is
exactly what these men did.

The specific charge—that Paul and Silas were advocating
unlawful customs—was untrue. Unlawful practices weren't part of
Paul and Silas's message. Their message and intent wasn't to per-
suade the citizens of Philippi to violate the customs of the Romans.
The city certainly wasn't in an uproar—other than the one being
caused by the men who'd lost their means of income. But because
Paul had driven the demonic spirit from this girl, they were going
to pay. They were seized, dragged, accused, stripped, beaten
severely, and thrown into prison.

Our lives are like that. One event can change everything
dramatically, suddenly. A large door turns on small hinges. In
just a moment of time we can feel seized, dragged, and thrown
into an unexpected time of confinement—all of life restricted by

the turn of events. A driver crosses the center divide, and with the sound of squealing tires as metal crunches against metal, life is never the same. A young girl dives into the bottom of a swimming pool, and she never walks again. The phone rings with news that shakes life to its core. These things can and do happen. Sometimes when things seem to be so good, they can quickly become so bad.

Sentenced. Beaten. Secluded. Bound. It wasn't enough to make Paul and Silas suffer the indignity of a racially tainted kangaroo court. No due process of law and determining of guilt, just a sentencing on the basis of false accusations. It wasn't enough that they were beaten to such a degree that even in the barbarism of their day, it's described as a "severe" beating. No, there was more to come. It seemed right in the minds of their accusers and the magistrates that Paul and Silas would also be secluded and bound.

They were thrown into prison. No prisoners' rights advocates were around to ensure proper treatment. Like garbage tossed into a pit, these two emissaries of the Most High God were thrown into the inner prison, the most secure dungeon in the prison complex. It was a horrible place, a cell dug deep into the earth, dark and damp with the moisture of an earthen floor. And it stunk with the odor of human refuse. The pungent odor of urine burned the nostrils. Secured in the stocks, they couldn't even move from the place where the guards had thrown them. And the guards faced few restraints concerning how they treated prisoners in their care.

So it was for Paul and Silas. A powerful ministry led to a prison cell.

The same can happen to us. While our experience may not be ministry that leads to a prison cell, in an instant our lives can change for what appears to be the worst. One day a pastor commented to his congregation, "There's a truth here we must understand. Bad things do happen to good people. If we don't understand this truth, we'll be forever asking, 'Why?' It's how we react to the bad things that counts."[1]

A Praise and Prayer Service

IN THE DARKNESS of the prison, the sound of two voices could be heard. It wasn't the moaning of beaten men or curses directed against their captors and tormentors. Instead, Paul and Silas sang words of praise. There in the prison cell they held a praise service! "When a train goes through a tunnel and it gets dark," Corrie ten Boom wrote, "you don't throw away the ticket and jump off. You sit still and trust the engineer."[2]

They sang! When the night was the darkest, they sang the loudest—maybe not in volume but in power. The sound of their vocals pierced the silence of a jail in Philippi. One commentator points out that singing is "a time-tested method of responding to suffering" because "singing helps us focus on the glorious eternal realities that may be clouded by the gloomy temporary realities. It helps us especially because, when we cannot produce words of our own, we can use the words of others."[3]

The bottom line is this: Paul and Silas worshiped when it hurt.

We may want to ask, "How could they?" Worship—or at least the appearance of it—comes easy in air-conditioned buildings with padded pews. But it seems unimaginable in a dark, damp, and smelly prison. We're accustomed to easing into worship services, slipping into a familiar seat. But even then our thoughts often may be filled with almost everything but God. Isn't that how we often go to church? We're kind of there, kind of not. Watch the clock, figure out what to wear, pick up your Bible, jump into the car, and head down the road for church. Your mind races—barely into your seat but already leaving worship in the dust as the rest of the day's activities loom ahead. You're dreading the week ahead, a cloud of anticipation so large and gloomy that even a choir anthem with orchestra accompaniment barely dents the predisposition of your brain.

Some might even be thankful to live in a day of caffeinated Christianity. Nice people with servant hearts and alarms that go off early even on a Sunday are staffing the Koinonia Café in the lobby or manning the pots in the adult fellowship room. And if the coffee won't do the trick, perhaps a shot of sugar in the form of a crème-filled pastry will help. Their prayer could even be, "A little help here, Lord, because my mind has not joined my body."

A gently spoken "Good Morning" will suffice to start shifting their gears to the church mode. Some nice words, welcoming thoughts, and the required dose of announcements push them out of first and into second gear. Now the focus is starting to sharpen. It is church time—and the habits begin to fire up, hitting on more cylinders, not just sputtering like a car in need of a tune-up on a cold winter morning. Thankful for routine, they stand, sit, pray, sing, give, listen, pray, and leave.

Sadly, far too often this is the way we worship. It appears to be more gerbil than human, running through the habit trails of church. Probably all of us have had that kind of church experience.

But none of this was taking place in the prison setting of Paul and Silas. Their praise wasn't linked to the quality of the music, the comfort of the surroundings, the acceptability of the worship style or the speaking abilities of the pastor.

They sang.

Praise, not just singing but true praise of God, pulls our eyes off the circumstances we find ourselves in and directs our gaze to the One who is worthy of all praise. Our songs remind us of the truth that God is good. Our temporary world is a mess—a sin-sick, sin-cursed world. And God calls us to remember that eternity is permanent. By His grace and for His glory we'll get through this temporary life. So we sing—not the blues, but songs of praise. And our songs remind us of this truth: God is good.

When we read about Paul and Silas, we need to remember that what they did then we can do now. Our worship can't be confined only to good times. We must expand it to the "all" times. God's goodness isn't dependent upon our circumstances and our praise shouldn't be either.

Perhaps that night in prison, Job came to Paul's mind. In our times of difficulty, most of us are quick to remember Job. It was probably the same with people in the first-century church. Job's reversal of fortunes was well known; and now, once again, Paul and Silas were experiencing the same kind of sudden, downward change. And like Job, they worshiped.

We'll all experience the goodness of God in ways we deem "good" and also in times that we'd prefer not to experience at all. Yet in both the good times and the bad times we must recognize God at work as did Job. He said to his wife, "Shall we accept good from God, and not trouble?" (Job 2:10) The best of times had become the worst of times for this man, whom the Bible calls "the greatest man among all the people of the East" (1:3). And in the worst of times "he fell to the ground in worship and said: 'Naked I came from my mother's womb, and naked I will depart. The LORD gave and the LORD has taken away; may the name of the LORD be praised" (1:20-21).

In his final column after more than twenty years of writing for *Eternity* magazine, Joseph Bayly brought together the themes of the severity of God and the goodness of God. He and his wife had suffered greatly in the deaths of three of their children. Then he recounted God's grace in the lives of each of his four living children. He wrote, "Mary Lou and I are aware that all this represents the grace of God, but also that for ourselves and our children the road hasn't ended. Yet we know that both by his severity and by his goodness God has shown consistent faithfulness. God is good. He is worthy of all truth and all glory. Amen."[4]

When Paul and Silas met Lydia, it was easy to say, "Praise the Lord." When the slave girl was delivered from demonic possession, again it was easy to say, "Praise the Lord." When guards then fastened chains on their legs and turned the key to lock their cells, they still said, "Praise the Lord." Was it easy? It probably took great effort, an effort that lifted their eyes from their circumstances and to the One who is always worthy of praise. God was still good and worthy of their praise, even then.

But here's the glitch—the thing that can keep you from praising God from the cell you find yourself in: Your mind has the incredible ability not just to reason, but also to record and replay. In stressful times, our brains seem to get stuck on replay. Even your sleep, if it comes at all, is interrupted as your mind replays the hurts. Over and over, it plays anticipated conversations, hoped-for outcomes, the things you wanted. Or perhaps it just replays the hurt. Soon it feels like your brain is trapped, unable to break free from the memories. Your mind and emotions are caught in an inescapable downward spiral, going over and over and over . . . lower into the depths of your mental prison.

You need to swap out the tape! Hit the eject button! Put in a different CD! Exit out of that program! Sure, it's easier to stay slumped in the recliner, which becomes an emotional decliner. Yes, it takes effort to make the change. But consider the direction you're headed: downward. Things aren't going to look any better from farther down in the pit.

Of course, God doesn't want you to become some kind of "Don't Worry, Be Happy" detached-from-reality bubblehead. But He does want the truth about Him and His goodness to be the focus of your thoughts. So replace the replaying of your pain with the sounds of His praise. That might mean literal singing. Or you may just need to change the tracks on the brain's CD, choosing to focus on the good things of God. Will this cure all that ails you? No, but it's an important first step in breaking out of the darkness.

You awaken. It's the middle of the night and the room is dark. As you look around the room, your eyes search for light—any light. Perhaps the faint glow of a star peeking through the curtain will be just enough to help you get your bearings, to plan your steps. A little light in a dark room is all you need.

Remember to sing. In the darkest time, praise may be the little light you need to help you plan your steps out of that prison. You've seen what Paul and Silas did. Choose what you will do.

Choose to sing.

Study Guide

Part 1 — Getting into the Word

Prayer: As you begin this study, ask God to speak to you through His Word. Make it your goal not only to learn what the Bible has to say about God's goodness, but to understand what it means for you. Ask God to help you have a heart that always says, "God is good," a heart that will sing even in the dark times.

Reading and Hearing God's Word: Read Acts 16:6-40. Watch for verses or ideas that are especially meaningful to you. In particular, look for things that relate to the key points of this lesson, things that would naturally bring praise, and the things that brought pain. As you read again of the singing in the cell, let God's Word begin to expand your understanding of worship and its importance in difficult times.

Understanding God's Word: Read Acts 16:6-40 again. Underline key phrases or ideas. Then answer the following questions:
1. Other than the two major events of the powerful ministry in Philippi, what did Paul and Silas experience that would encourage them to praise God?
2. Summarize the turn in events, noting in particular the things that contributed to their imprisonment.

Meditating on God's Word: Write a brief summary of a verse or idea that was meaningful to you from this passage.

Part 2 — Taking the Word into My World

We like hammock times. Perhaps you're going through one of those times now or you remember one from the past. Describe one of those periods when praise came easily.

Now think about the parking-lot times. Those may come to mind even more quickly or may be reality for you right now. How did that hard time affect your relationship with God and your worship of Him?

Perhaps you're familiar with the story of Job, but you've never focused on the praise Job offered. Read Job 1:20-21 and compare his situation with Paul and Silas's prison time.

The last sentence of this chapter is the first lesson of this book. "Choose to sing" helps us remember that God is good even when our situation isn't.

Part 3 — Grabbing Hold
Close your time of study by quietly worshiping God in prayer and praise. Praise Him for who He is, not just for what He does. Ask that He will help you maintain a heart of praise. Perhaps there's a song of praise that you'd like to offer to God as an act of worship right now.

HERE COMES TROUBLE —
HAVE FAITH

HABAKKUK

The three years they waited to begin their family didn't seem like too much time. Their wedding ceremony followed their college graduations. Then back to the same campus for graduate work. She had studied missions and he was "pre-sem," undergraduate slang for someone heading to seminary for further training. Their aim was to serve God in missions.

When they decided the time was right for a child, the first pregnancy came easily. It gave no hint of the struggle that lay ahead—a struggle with infertility. Up to this point in their lives, everything made sense and was moving forward as planned. But their optimism would soon be replaced with uncertainty and perplexity. They could easily replace worship with the question, "Why?" The song gave way to sorrow.

A low-level concern replaced the initial elation of expecting their first child. At eleven weeks, Julie experienced some slight, almost unmentionable bleeding. Perhaps spurred by the uncertainties of a first-time pregnancy, she went to see the doctor and a series of tests followed. Technicians took ultrasounds. Then Julie and her husband, Michael, sat stunned as they were told that their baby didn't have a heartbeat and Julie would soon miscarry.

One day, a shower stall became a prayer room as Julie's tears started to flow, joining the rivulets of water from the spray in her face. Her crying became her praying as Julie turned her grief over to God, surrendering to His leading in their life together. "God, You are always right and always good," she prayed. "I don't understand why this is happening, but I know that You are always right and that I can trust You." Then her prayer ventured into territory that most would avoid: "Lord, even if You never allow us to have children, You're still right and You're still good." A deluge of tears followed, ones that she would later say she did not understand.

Sometimes We Live Perplexed

"WHEN I'M FOLLOWING you, God, I feel a bit lost most of the time. But that makes sense. I'm not leading you. You're leading me." That was the opening line in an update from a friend who serves as a missionary in South Africa. He'd come across that statement in a book on strategic planning. He and a group of others who had joined in a church planning effort were reading it as a guide for their times of mapping out the direction of their work.

The first half of that quote strikes home immediately! We know that life is filled with times of feeling lost—that sense that you're going somewhere, but you're just not sure where. It's like you unknowingly took a wrong turn, and as the scenery slowly changes from familiar to unfamiliar, you begin to develop a gnawing feeling of uncertainty. You have a growing sense of error. Finally you admit, "I think we're lost." The whole experience makes you feel like you've just been marinated in a sauce made up of exasperation and confusion.

"So, just where am I and where am I going?" you ask yourself—and if you're a guy, you ask *only* yourself because real men don't ask for directions! A delay along the family vacation route is one thing; those periods of life when you feel lost are another. Sometimes it doesn't take much to have that "a bit lost" feeling make its presence known.

The Perplexity of Life

A DOCTOR CAN give it to you and you don't even need to be able to read the handwriting on the prescription pad—just hearing the words "I think we better run some tests" can make you feel like a scout has been practicing square knots on the cords of your stomach. "The market's not very good right now," says the manager at work. And at that point you can't imagine any ship on the sea sinking faster or deeper than what just happened in the pit of your stomach.

It could even be that nothing, just *nothing* in and of itself, makes you feel "a bit lost." Nothing's happening, nothing's changing, nothing is going on except the routine. Routines can be comfortable but they can also feel like ruts—which someone described as a grave with the ends kicked out. The "same old, same old" can easily feel like bars that slowly but surely establish themselves, caging you in, imprisoning you. Prisoners in physical cells know that an unchanging routine can rob them of all hope. Others find the same desperation outside of prison walls, but trapped inside walls built by discouragement.

Even when we're following God, we can feel a bit lost. We may be confused by what we see around us. We impatiently want it to change for the better right now and can even be exasperated by it all. That is real life—life lived not just in the fast lane but in the "lost" lane. And the more we're perplexed by life, the more likely we'll do the natural thing—not necessarily logical but definitely natural—and complain.

It just doesn't make sense, until we realize we're not leading God but He's leading us. This realization that comes by faith in the unseen but ever-present God. We finally shake our feeling of lostness when we understand that the eternal God is leading us. Learning that, accepting it, and living it can take time.

Friends tried to help Michael and Julie: "At least you know you can get pregnant. You're young and still have time." They did still trust the Lord, but began to expect those words of well-meaning friends to come true. Instead, three long years followed. And they discovered a different type of pain—waiting.

Those years included tests, treatments, hormone therapy for both Michael and Julie, and finally a second pregnancy. This time the thrill was tempered by previous experience and again, at eleven weeks, an ultrasound confirmed that they had lost their second child. The night before they'd listened to a simple, straightforward message: "God is good—all the time." They went away encouraged and strengthened in their faith, but also with a sense of apprehension.

They had the same technician as three years before. Obviously saddened by what the tests revealed, he reluctantly shared the news with them that they'd lost another baby. "This was not a time to push God out, blaming Him for my pain," Julie wrote. "It was a time to turn to Him and allow Him to wrap His arms around me and comfort His child."

In the days ahead they learned another difficult reality, a genetic disorder called a balanced translocation of the sixth and twenty-first chromosomes. To them it sounded like they would never have children. The reality, according to their doctor, was that it would be difficult to have children. They'd likely lose more children to miscarriage if they continued to try. A genetic counselor gave them the miserable odds: a fifty/fifty chance of losing every pregnancy and an overall twenty percent chance of carrying all the way to the end of the pregnancy and then losing their child.

Remember these words? "When I'm following you, God, I feel a bit lost most of the time. But that makes sense. I'm not leading you. You're leading me." It's easier to say some lessons than to learn them, and this was definitely one of those for Michael and Julie. They were now in "school," not just seminary, but a place in life where God teaches lessons that run counter to popular thought, and where His lesson plans are nothing like what we would design. "One thing we know," they would tell you, is that "God is good— all the time. He's good and He's right, and He'll comfort our souls and use our pain to change the lives of others, if we let Him. It's so comforting to know that God doesn't waste anything—including our tears."

Out of their time of feeling lost, Michael and Julie came to understand that they weren't leading God; He was leading them. While this wasn't a "happy-ever-after ending," it was a good ending, one where peace replaces pain, acceptance overcomes apprehension, and following erases wondering and wandering.

Not everyone learns this lesson so well. Some take a rather difficult path in this special school where God teaches tough lessons. Some people head into what seems to be the logical direction, into times of complaint—or they distance themselves from God, from the One they need to draw near to in such a confusing time.

The Perplexity of Habakkuk's Day

IN HIS WORD, God gives us real-life examples, people who were flesh and blood, people who felt "a bit lost" at times and totally lost other times. Like we often do, these people did the natural thing: they complained. But God doesn't give us these examples just so we can say, "Boy, I know the feeling!" He gives them so we can learn how to grow from that feeling of lostness to realize that He's leading us. And we *can* grow—if we allow God and His Word to take root in our hearts, live it out in our lives, and take another step out of our cells of discouragement. This step could be called, "Have Faith."

Among the twelve books in the Old Testament that are known as the Minor Prophets, none is more significant than Habakkuk. Theologians describe these books as "minor" not because their messages are less important, but because of their lengths.

Habakkuk's name means "embracer." Perhaps he was the kind of guy that you'd run into in the foyer of the church, and he'd give you a hug. Or maybe people called him "embracer" because of his love for God. Perhaps his love for God was so great that his name is a statement—an assessment of his person—and people simply described him this way. And have you ever noticed that people who strongly love God also love people, embracing both? Habakkuk may have been like that, embracing God and embracing the people of God. The nation of Israel needed both in the days that lay ahead. They needed to know the love of God and they needed a person like Habakkuk to be the embodiment of that love. Their sovereignty as a nation was about to end. The army of Babylon, led by king Nebuchadnezzar, was poised to invade Judah, to lay siege to the city of Jerusalem—and ultimately he was victorious. Nebuchadnezzar's troops killed, captured, and deported the people as slaves and ruined the city. It was a time for an "embracer" to make his presence known—not only to give that reassuring hug from a friend, but to point the hurting people back to God.

This whole situation perplexed Habakkuk for two reasons. The first came from his own impatience. He didn't understand why God didn't do something about the situation in Israel. Things were a mess! Violence, injustice, crooked lawyers, and selfish politicians filled his world. And God seemed to be doing nothing about it— about any of it! That was the core of his first complaint.

His second complaint sprung from exasperation. When God told Habakkuk that He was using the Babylonians to deal with Israel, the prophet was incredulous. "You're going to do what!" he might have exclaimed. It just didn't make sense.

His ministry came at an opportune time, but one with great challenge. How could he say, "God is good" when the nation had fallen, the capital had been destroyed, and its citizens enslaved?

The Needed Perspective

HERE'S THE ANSWER to how: You live by your faith.

Imagine in the midst of desperate times—the entrapping, imprisoning times of difficulty—that you feel a hug from dear friends, hear a whisper in your ear, and sense a truth in your mind by their words. They softly repeat a sentence that doesn't explode in your soul but slowly takes root and grows. They say, "The righteous will live by their faith." That's what Habakkuk whispers to us.

36

Perhaps when the armies came and even after the people of Israel became slaves, Habakkuk reminded them of this truth. And we know that before the armies came, this man from God prepared the people of God with the truth. He reminded them that we don't live on the basis of what we see, what we experience, or what delights us. We live by faith in God.

Did that just slip by you? Some truths of Scripture are like the familiar objects along the side of a road you travel often. You're so accustomed to seeing these landmarks that you don't even notice them. Take for example Psalm 23. You can read it and miss all of its meaning. You read the first sentence, and your mind goes on autopilot as you think, "I know this one," and your eyes glaze as they pass over the printed words. Or consider the times you recite the Lord's prayer but don't even notice the words or phrases.

Martin Luther thundered these words: "The righteous will live by faith!" and it caught people's attention. But we've heard this story so often that our minds head down the same path, thinking the issue is salvation. And we miss the truth, the golden nugget that can erase our perplexity and give us the perspective we need to survive — even thrive — in the confines of difficult times, and lead us to liberating times of praise.

Thunder these words! They're crucial. "The righteous will live by faith!" They contain the truth we need. I don't want to say something like "Learn the secret of this phrase" because there's nothing secret about it! God put it in the book, in plain type, for us to learn. So write it down now. Seriously. Stop reading. Get a pen. Find some place and write down the "secret." Put it on an index card you use as a bookmark, inside the cover of this book, or using lipstick on the mirror of your bathroom. Just write it down and in time you'll realize the truth of this statement.

Here it is: "The righteous will live by his faith" (Habakkuk 2:4).

That's it. The not-so-secret "secret." It's the key that can unlock your understanding, that can move you from complaint to calmness and from perplexity to the perspective you need on the events of your life. And if you give it a little think-time, if you work at understanding this single verse from Habakkuk, God will show you that life isn't a matter of living with the feeling that you're a bit lost most of the time, but of understanding that He is leading us.

We readily identify with Habakkuk's perplexity, found in the first chapter of the book that bears his name. He didn't understand why God wasn't doing something about the mess the nation of Israel was in. Then he didn't understand why God would use the Babylonians to deal with the situation. But ultimately, Habakkuk's perplexity is replaced with a perspective on how God wants us to live in times of confusion and feeling trapped within the cells of our circumstances. We must live by faith.

As one commentator put it, "God did not give Habakkuk a philosophical answer to the problem of suffering. Humans must live by faith in God, who is ultimately just and in control of history. Even when some events seem to contradict this belief, we are to trust in God."[1] So take this truth, break it into bite-size pieces, absorb it in its entirety.

"The Righteous"

Without a doubt, this phrase tightens the parameters. While it may be popular and appealing to think that all of God's truth is for all people, it's not. The truth in this verse is specifically for people that God pronounces as "The righteous." Not all are! Just read all of Habakkuk 2:4 and it will be readily apparent. Some people are "puffed up." They're proud people who trust in themselves. The Chaldeans were such, puffed up by their victories, not realizing that it was God who enabled them to conquer. They thought it was by their own strength, and Habakkuk said that strength is what they considered to be their god. They were wrong. Their victories were the work of God. They just didn't know it, and their pride would keep them from knowing it.

Pride can keep people from heaven because forgiveness isn't attained by accomplishments, but by humility. We humble ourselves before God, receive what He so freely offers, a gift given not because we deserve it but because of His grace. As the hymn writer put it, "Jesus paid it all, all to Him I owe." Proud people can't admit that it is all of grace and none of themselves. So for this truth from Habakkuk to work in your life, you must be of the group of people who humble themselves because they trust in the Lord.

Someone has said that this text is the Mount Everest in the biblical understanding of salvation. It's huge—and the summit unattainable to the proud. But the request of the humble is granted immediately, and salvation through Christ is theirs. Some who seek acceptance with God look for what they can do. That makes sense to them—do something and God will smile! But God says all that needs to be done has been, by Jesus. The simplicity of faith strikes at the heart of pride, leaving nothing for boasting. When we replace effort with simple trust, we attain salvation.

"Will Live"

There's a future sense to this phrase. One day, our lives on this earth will come to an end. But death isn't truly the end. As one eloquent speaker stated it, death isn't a period but a comma. We will live, forever.

There's also an immediate, present-tense aspect to the words "will live." The words that follow tell *how* God wants us to live! Our actions aren't a human effort to meet some standard that gains God's favor. Rather, we're to aim our lives in the direction of God's choosing, living the way He wants us to live. Put simply, faith isn't a one-time act but a way of life. It begins with faith in Jesus Christ and then becomes the core of a life lived with God's blessing.

The pieces of paper on the desk were a variety of bright colors, all folded over. They were small notes handed to me by a prisoner when I'd returned to preach at the State Correctional Institute. He knew the reality of a cell and the reality of freedom in Christ. My prison right then was so different—his of literal bars, mine of current circumstances.

I unfolded a lavender-colored note and read, "I call on the Lord in my distress, and he answers me. Psalm 120:1." *How could he know I needed that verse?* I thought. I opened a peach-colored one next: "Cheer up! God has His hand on you and is not going to leave you stranded. He who hath begun a good work in you will continue. See 1 Thessalonians 5:24." Just a few weeks before, I'd returned to the church behind the wall to minister the Word to the men there. Now one of those men ministered to me with his notes.

On the green paper the prisoner had written, "Let the morning bring me word of your unfailing love, for I have put my trust in you. Show me the way I should go, for to you I lift up my soul. Psalm 143:8." Another note said, "Great peace have they who love your law, and nothing can make them stumble. Psalm 119:165." This prisoner had even given me a prayer for today: "Dear God, help us to view trials as opportunities to glorify you through our faith, leaning on your love and protection. In Jesus' name. Amen. Read Psalm 119:145-152."

Scraps of paper. Handed to fellow prisoners. Handed to me. Reminders that the Word is to affect the way I live. Today. Now.

"By Faith"

It would seem to go without saying that to live "by faith" doesn't mean "by sight." But sometimes people overlook the obvious. They say "by faith," but then they live on the basis of what they see, limiting their hope, their understanding, their perspectives to only what they can observe.

So God gives Habakkuk something to really think about. Everything around him looks like a mess. Everything headed his direction looks even worse. The day is approaching when the city of God, Jerusalem, will be laid waste by the Babylonians. And God says, "For the earth will be filled with the knowledge of the glory of the LORD, as the waters cover the sea" (Habakkuk 2:14). Now think about that. There's no evidence to support this statement, and there's plenty of evidence to the contrary. Unless you live by faith.

And one more thing. "The LORD is in his holy temple; let all the earth be silent before him" (Habakkuk 2:20). God is still on the throne. No use complaining or even doubting because this is for sure. He still rules and overrules. It may have seemed to Habakkuk that God wasn't interested in what was going on. But He was. And He still is. It may have seemed that God wasn't working in the world at all, but He was. And He still is, in His own time.

This is why the just live by faith. Living by what we see is discouraging. Living by faith is encouraging. It helps us understand the truth that God is good, all the time.

The imagery in the closing verses of the book of Habakkuk is agricultural. As we picture the reality of the scene described, it's easy to see how discouraging the situation was. No buds on the fig trees, no grapes on the vines, no olive crops. The fields barren, producing no food. Even the livestock are depleted. There are neither sheep in the pen nor cattle in the stalls. Fruit-bearing trees and vines, fields, flocks, and herds—all gone, all barren, all desolate. It was a time of great material loss.

Think of this with a farmer's mind-set. He makes his living with fig trees, and then one day the trees just don't bud. On top of that, no grapes are on the vines. He's dependent on producing crops and when that doesn't happen, he fears he won't make it. And he knows that the people dependent on him for food will find sky-rocketing prices as supply diminishes and demand increases.

Not only are the fields affected, but so are the flocks and herds. A dairyman builds his herd, as does a stockman. They plan ahead for the next season when the calves will be born to replenish the herd. But when the stalls and pens are empty, all is gone—including hope for next season. The farmer is facing total economic ruin.

This difficulty wasn't just for the unjust. It affected everyone. The prophet himself was in the middle of all of this. He experienced the economic downturn, the food shortages, the fear for their safety, the anticipated fall of the city into the hands of a feared and ruthless enemy. Everyone—righteous and unrighteous—suffered.

Most of us are aware that we sometimes focus too much on the material things we have or our needs, wants, and wishes. But rarely do we think long about the possibility of losing it all. That's not a pretty picture, and it doesn't fit our idea of how God is supposed to bless His children. Yet it can, and it does, happen. In all ages, some of the best people have been found in destitute circumstances. It happened to Job. While Job's story is so familiar to many of us, he still provides a great example, one we shouldn't overlook. Translate the agricultural terms of Job into our language. His camels were his transportation fleet. His oxen were his farm implements, his servants were his employees, his flocks and herds were his "stock portfolio." And he lost it all! His financial empire was destroyed, his family decimated by death, and even his own health took a downward spiral. One day, the greatest man of the East found himself standing beside ten fresh graves wondering why.

The answer God ultimately gave Job is the same answer He gave Habakkuk and that He gives us. Essentially He said, "I am God. You're not. You need to trust Me." And Job did. In the last chapter of the book that bears his name, Job comes to realize this truth. When God answered Job, He didn't answer the specific question but gave Job a glimpse of His power and greatness. When God finished speaking, Job was speechless. God is God. We're not. He's in control. We're not. He says, "Trust Me." We must.

The Resulting Praise

HABAKKUK REALIZES THIS truth and has even more to say, words we need to grab hold of to help us in the dark days when the worst has come—days that entrap and confine us. Though all these things happen, Habakkuk says, "yet I will rejoice in the LORD, I will be joyful in God my Savior" (Habakkuk 3:18). In God, he says, he will find his strength, a strength that he compares to that of a deer, a strength that will allow that deer to scale the heights of a mountain with a sure-footed confidence.

The sound of a foghorn woke me early one morning. It wasn't a loud blast, just a soft sound, muffled and distant. Our cabin on the ship had a television set in it, with a channel broadcasting the view from the bow of the ship, twenty-four hours a day. I turned on the TV, switched to that channel, and saw the reason for the ship's foghorn. You couldn't see beyond the bow more than a few feet.

In fear, I could have rushed to the front of the ship, leaned over the rail, scanning the waters ahead in hopes of seeing, in hopes of helping navigate the ship. But it would have been useless to do so—and it was unnecessary. The captain of the ship knew what to do and we sailed on safely. Instead, I turned off the TV—my curiosity satisfied that we were indeed in a fog—rolled over, and went back to sleep.

The events of life may be as impenetrable to understanding as that fog was to my eyes. Yet we must remember that God is good. Live by faith and trust Him. Live by faith not dependent upon circumstances, but upon God.

A tornado hits. We stand in the midst of the rubble. If we live by sight, all we can see is rubble. No hope, no help, no praise—because on the basis of what we can see, it doesn't appear that "God is good."

The righteous don't live by what they see with their eyes but by what they know in their hearts. They live by faith. To live by faith doesn't mean that we know the answers to our questions, or that we know the reasons, understand the events, or like the consequences of the situations we're in. It does mean we have a willingness to say, "God is in control and I'll trust Him. I'll look beyond the immediate to the eternal."

Look at the closing verses of Habakkuk's story and see that he was a follower of God who knew what to do with his problems. But remember, it wasn't always that way. Earlier we learned a key word that described the prophet: *perplexed*. First he was perplexed that God wasn't doing anything about the injustice in the land. Then God changed his perspective.

The difference when you live by faith? The tornado hits. You're standing in the midst of the rubble, and all you see around you is ruin. The wind has died down. In the quieter moments, as you survey the devastation, some sounds slightly intrude into your thoughts. You hear the sirens of emergency vehicles off in the distance. A piece of flashing, the thin metal that before protected the eaves of your house, is now creaking as it twists in the wind, torn loose and hanging like a stiff rag from the nail the wind didn't quite rip out of the wood.

And there are footsteps. Someone comes up next to you, but your emotions are too frayed to look and the storm has exhausted your supply of fear. Then beside you stands a man whose face is one of understanding; he knows what you're feeling, the numbness of the brain that is trying to move beyond the shock of the moment. His arm reaches around your back as his hand rests on your shoulder and you feel that "side hug"—one given by a person standing beside you, so reaffirming, one that says so much in its silent pressure.

His head tilts slightly toward your ear and without taking his eyes off the devastation left by the storm he says one sentence: "The righteous will live by his faith." One more hug, and then Habakkuk walks away. The "embracer" has embraced you with more than a physical grasp. He has surrounded you with truth, given you the perspective you need so that you too can say, "God is good."

You can say that when you live by faith.

Study Guide

Part 1—Getting into the Word
Prayer: As you pray, ask God to help you understand why Habakkuk was so perplexed with Him first not doing anything and then doing something unimaginable. The better you understand how this didn't make sense to Habakkuk, the better you'll understand why his later perspective is so vital.

Reading and Hearing God's Word: Read the entire book of Habakkuk. It doesn't take that long. As you do, remember that chapter one is about his perplexity, chapter two is about his perspective, and chapter three centers on his praise. Look for the words and phrases that bring out these points.

Understanding God's Word: Go through the book of Habakkuk, one chapter at a time. This will mean a little longer study but it can

have great benefits. People often focus only on the key phrase —
Habakkuk 2:4 — or the ending praise of chapter three. So take your
time! Underline key phrases and ideas. Then tackle the following
assignment:

1. Scan Habakkuk 1, listing the prophet's complaints.
   What key words does he use? Do you ever complain to
   God using the same words?
2. The second chapter contains the great statement: "the
   righteous will live by his faith" (verse 4). But there's
   much more to the book than that. Think about how
   verses 14 and 20 fit with this verse.
3. What things that can go wrong are mentioned toward
   the end of the third chapter? What spiritual blessings are
   found in verses 18 and 19? Are those blessings because
   of or in spite of the things mentioned in verse 17?

Meditating on God's Word: Read the closing section, Habakkuk
3:17-19, and write a brief summary of these verses. Use words,
phrases, and examples that would challenge God's people today.

Part 2 — Taking the Word into My World

Grasping the important lesson of Habakkuk can come quickly: We
need to live by faith, not sight. But taking the time to see the message of the entire book can help cement that truth in our souls.
Also, it becomes clear that the prophet was writing during a dark
time, but was encouraged by the truth that we live by faith, not
sight. Consider the following, to bring this certainty home to your
own experience.

1. Compare your life with the first chapter. List things that
   perplex you, that give you reason to complain to God.
2. What are things that could discourage you today, similar
   to the agricultural disasters listed in Habakkuk 3:17?
3. It's easy to begin a testimony of praise with the words, "I
   praise God because of . . . " Habakkuk could have said,
   "I praise God in spite of . . . " What's the difference
   between these two phrases?

Part 3 — Grabbing Hold

Now redo the assignment in the "Meditating on God's Word" section. This time make it personal and real by rewriting it in the first person. Write your prayer of praise and ask God to help you live by faith.

SINGING IN THE PAIN — REMEMBER

PSALM 137

S ometimes it's easy to sing and sometimes it's not. At times the words just flow, like water cascading over a dam—not a trickle or a gushing foam spraying out over the river below, but a steady, thick, ripple-less, clear slab of water effortlessly cresting the spillway and falling serenely in its unimpeded journey to the sea. Our words in those times come easily; we sing the song, holding nothing back, nothing hindering it—the praise just flows.

Then we face the other times, or perhaps better said, the rest of the time. "Some days I can throw a tomato through a brick wall," a baseball pitcher once remarked. "And other days I couldn't dent a pane of glass with a rock." In those days, the words don't flow. We can't seem to sing the songs or even utter the praise because we can't get the words to start. Everything going on in our lives, everything in our hearts, everything in our minds, and everything around us seems to be saying, "Don't sing; be quiet; stop the music." In those moments, it can be so hard to say, "God is good." Sometimes, as a songwriter put it, "living takes the life out of you."

You turn the key
Then close the door behind you
Drop your bags on the floor

You reach for the light
But there's darkness deep inside
And you can't take it anymore
'Cause sometimes living takes the life out of you
And sometimes living is all you do.[1]

Evidence that life is hard is abundant for a prisoner in a physical cell. The key is turned every day, not by them but for them, locking them in. Forget the ads about what mattress will give you the best night's sleep, because it doesn't come in prison-bunk size. Don't wonder about where to eat that next special dinner out because every meal is mass-produced—edible but not much else—eaten in a cafeteria that may put food on the tray, but that's as far as it goes. The sights, sounds, smells, and schedule of day-to-day existence are constant reminders of the consequences of breaking the law, of punishment intended to fit the crime, to change the criminal. Life is hard there.

Life can be hard outside the walls also. Maybe the mattress is the best possible, the food selection enviable, and the lifestyle one that looks good in every way—yet you feel like you're in a prison. Events can change your emotions and your emotions can chain your soul. Your life doesn't resemble the advertised "good life," the way of living that is supposed to be so available to all.

In an odd way, our culture acknowledges that life isn't so great by advertisements that promise to make it so. Ads strike where people are in life. "This is what you need," they cry. "Here is what you want." Companies spend their advertising dollars and make their pitches, anticipating that people will make purchases to fill their needs, satisfy their wants, enhance their status, and ease their pain.

Brand-name prescription drugs show up in ads with increasing frequency. Patients call their doctors, asking for a specific medication because the ad they just saw offers both diagnosis and treatment in thirty seconds or less. Relief in tablet form or easy-to-swallow gelcap. They even ask for depression and anxiety medications by name.

Life is hard. So our culture accepts—even demands—relief in the form of a pill. Life really is hard, and the pain of existence seems intolerable at times. At least an inmate knows the length of his sentence or the date of his parole hearing. But the other prisons people are confined to have no calendar or court docket to suggest an end in sight.

You Can't Sing If You Forget the Words

Not too many people argue when you say life is hard. You probably know it, you've experienced it, or you're in a hard time right now.

Say "God is good" on the other hand, and some might argue. They'll say, "If God's so good, then why has this young mother been diagnosed with cancer, and why are her children facing the reality of her funeral?" "If God's so good, why didn't He stop the hijackers, why did He let thousands of innocent people die in the World Trade Center, in the Pentagon, and on that rural hillside in Pennsylvania?" "If God's so good, why am I experiencing this pain that won't go away?" "God is good and I have been laid off. How do you figure that!" And the list goes on.

And there is no song, no word of praise, no ability or desire to say, "God is good." The jury may be out but the evidence is in. Life is hard and we're not sure that God is all that good. No song, no singing.

The reality is, there are times we can't sing.

Paul and Silas could sing in prison but we can't. Habakkuk could say, "the righteous will live by his faith," but we struggle with that. Some can praise God "in spite of" but we can't. We can't praise God without good reason, reason we judge to be good. Sometimes there's no song. So, welcome to the club! As one songwriter did put it,

Life is hard, the world is cold
We're barely young and then we're old.[2]

49

The Singer Who Couldn't Sing

Can't sing—except maybe the blues? Nothing new with that. Even one of the writers of the Psalms knew a time when he couldn't either—he just hung up his harp. A word of warning: we're about to hit bottom. The words he wrote aren't encouraging words, nor is the situation of this man of God. It's bleak; it's real life. But keep this in mind: It may be the bottom, but it's not the final scene. God allows us to hear the heart cry of this man for a reason. He's letting us know that we're not alone in our times of discouragement and that we're not condemned to live the rest of our lives surrounded by an inky darkness that blocks our vision and stains our souls. He gives us a vital step, one that keeps us from total despair and helps us move back to the light.

But first, the psalmist's lament:

> *By the rivers of Babylon we sat and wept*
> *when we remembered Zion.*
> *There on the poplars*
> *we hung our harps,*
> *for there our captors asked us for songs,*
> *our tormentors demanded songs of joy;*
> *they said, "Sing us one of the songs of Zion!"*
> *How can we sing the songs of the* LORD
> *while in a foreign land?* (Psalm 137:1-4)

He was a musician, possibly from the temple in Jerusalem, the Carnegie Hall of Israel. He was one of the best, in the best place, doing what he loved. The temple was a glorious place, its beauty unrivaled. And never before had music made such a significant contribution to worship. The shepherd who'd become king, the warrior who sat on the throne, the ruler who led the nation was also the writer of many psalms. Psalms had been used in worship before—but now, during David's reign, a new place was given to music, on a scale unparalleled before. Harps, cymbals, cornets, and trumpets now moved to the forefront as never before. Choirs led processions and times of celebration. Music sounded out.

When the Ark was brought to Jerusalem, there was music (see 2 Samuel 6:5). The plans for the temple included groups of singers and musicians who were a central part of the worship of God (see 1 Chronicles 25). The king himself was a contributor to the collection that would become the hymnbook of Israel—the Psalms. Those enduring, inspired writings that still resonate with worship and praise in our churches today and in our hearts.

The lives of temple musicians were filled with activities and excitement. The traffic of the nation passed through the city of Jerusalem as the people of God came to see the temple of their God. Noise, energy, crowds, celebration, sacrifices, praises, and praying filled their days. Scholars gathered, musicians interacted, pilgrims came, people worshiped—and the musicians were in the middle of it all, drinking it in from a front-row seat.

Jerusalem and its temple were the center of worship. It's hard for us to imagine the beauty of the temple. Solomon achieved his dream: a place to worship God, a place of grandeur and majesty. Of course, God's people can worship Him in any place—even in a tent, as the nation did during the wilderness wanderings. But the nation was no longer without a central temple. Artisans and craftsmen, enabled by the Holy Spirit, used the finest of materials to construct much more than a building. It was the temple of the living God, a structure that dominated the heights of the city of Jerusalem.

And everyone came there! Three times a year, God said, His people were to come to Jerusalem, to the temple. These would have been exciting events, prepared for in exacting detail, anticipated with great excitement. What could possibly be better than to be a musician there, in that place, at that time!

The songs flowed, the music filled the air, penetrating the hearts of those gathered to worship—but then it changed.

Why the Music Stopped

Remember, God had told Habakkuk that this day was coming, that the Babylonians would one day devastate the city of Jerusalem. He warned of the temple looted, people killed, and tens of thousands deported to a life of slavery in Babylon.

Read this and think, "World Trade Center." Think WTC but with a difference. There was no warning on September 11, 2001. It was a normal kind of day—clear skies, enjoyable temperatures, things to do, people to see, places to go. Then without warning a plane hit the north tower. The thought of terrorists flashed briefly. But then the second plane hit, and a third smashed into the Pentagon, and a fourth crashed into the hills of Stoney Creek, Pennsylvania. And then the terrorist warning light stayed on, burning brightly into the soul of a nation.

You remember where you were when you heard the news. You remember what you were doing when someone said, "A plane has hit the World Trade Center . . . another plane . . . another plane . . . another plane." It was an agonizing morning, and it's frozen in your memory not just because of the scale of the disaster but also the suddenness of it. That's what makes November 22, 1963, so indelible in the mind of a generation, or makes the words "the shuttle *Challenger*" bring up an instant mental image of a blue sky bisected by the contrail of a rocket, capped with the fury of an explosion.

For some reason, we can read accounts from the Bible without a sense of horror, without realizing the terror, without hearing the cries of grief from those who lost families and homes. The destruction of Jerusalem wasn't a terrorist attack, but a war of devastation. Read this and realize that this was real life for the writer of the psalm, real life that changed slowly, certainly, permanently.

The siege of Jerusalem lasted nearly six months. Day after day, the people of the city knew that it wasn't a matter of *if* something was going to happen, but *when*. The enemy army encircled the city and slowly squeezed the life out of Jerusalem. They cut off food supplies and threatened water supplies. Those within were under siege and would one day be under attack. In July of 586 B.C., the enemy army breached the city wall and poured through, flooding the streets with the sounds of war, destruction, and death. The king himself tried to escape but was captured and brought to Nebuchadnezzar. The enemy forced Zedekiah to witness the execution of his sons; then his captors blinded him so that the last thing he ever saw was the killing of his children. The Babylonians executed another eighty distinguished leaders, including the high priest Seraiah.

And then the captain of Nebuchadnezzar's bodyguard, Nebuzaradan, ordered the destruction of the temple and the looting of its remaining treasures. In the end, only the poorest of the people remained. The enemy took the rest of the survivors into captivity, a journey from Jerusalem that would be the antithesis of Jesus' Triumphal Entry years later. From the top of the Mount of Olives, Jesus would see spread before Him the beauty of Herod's temple, a city bursting with life and activity, joyous crowds gathered to celebrate Passover. But these refugees of war who journeyed away from Jerusalem would look over their shoulders at the smoldering ruins: the royal palace, the temple, and the city that had been destroyed. It symbolized the destruction of their way of life.

Life would never be the same. Perhaps as many as seventy thousand began that long desert trek to Babylon. Men of valor now marched as prisoners of war. Strong and fit craftsmen and smiths, now empty-handed, put foot in front of foot and followed the dusty path into captivity, where their skills and abilities would be used to serve their conquerors. People of wealth, whose slightest whims had been the concern of a staff of servants, were now at the mercy of the whims of their captors. Others couldn't keep up with the pace of this mass of dejected humanity as starvation and disease decimated their ranks; their bodies fell, lying as stark reminders to walk or die.

"Now sing!" was the taunt of the captors. They picked a man from the crowd. He wasn't a construction worker or a merchant, but a musician. He felt the cruelty of the captors in the stinging word, "Sing!" They mocked him, they mocked His God, who hadn't delivered Jerusalem from them, and they reveled in their superiority. "Sing!" they shouted—and the psalmist said, "I couldn't. I just hung my harp on the branch of a tree because I couldn't sing."

Instead, he sat and wept. His torment was real, the agony intense, and the words of the guards stung: "Sing me one of those songs you used to sing."

"How can we sing the songs of the LORD while in a foreign land?" (Psalm 137:4).

This psalmist is hurt and lonely. He's reached one of those low points of life. His only possession, perhaps, is his harp; his only asset his hope, and he didn't have much of that left. So he fills his writing with grief, anger, frustration, vindictiveness, patriotism, hatred, homesickness, torment, and with a love of Jerusalem and a loathing for Babylon. And he refuses to sing. He says, "How can I?"

That's life. Some days we just say, "I can't sing." We find ourselves in the same situation—frightened, our faith fragile. It's as if the God we thought would take care of us has let us down. Songs about His greatness, His love, His mercy don't bring comfort, only confusion and hurt.

For four days, Tom didn't have to face the world or deal with the torments of the downward spiral of his life. He'd been at the top with high level jobs in industry and ministry, but he'd recently begun to struggle with just wanting to live. It wasn't until the fifth day that he came to grips with his situation. That was the day he came out of the coma, the result of drinking the most potent poison he could find in his home, his second suicide attempt. This time he'd almost succeeded.

His first attempt with a kitchen knife had missed his heart by a fraction of an inch. The ambulance rushed him to the hospital, doctors performed emergency surgery to repair the physical damage, and Tom then spent time in a psychiatric ward. He went home but the depression remained.

This time it was a fall afternoon. The days had been filled with tension as his wife and daughter maintained a constant vigil, even forcing him to sleep between them at night, lest he should slip out of the bed unnoticed. Then the briefest of opportunities: he rushed down the stairs and into the garage. He grabbed an herbicide off the shelf and hurriedly opened it in hope that it would end his despair. Again the rush to the hospital. The trauma unit staff did not expect him to survive. Air-evacuated to a better-equipped facility where caregivers kept him alive. For four days Tom didn't have to deal with life. There was no song. Like Tom, like the psalmist, there are days when we just can't sing.

> *You start to cry*
> *'Cause you've been strong too long*
> *And that's not how you feel*
> *You try to pray*
> *But there's nothing left to say*
> *So you just quietly kneel.*[3]

The Return of the Song

> "We wept . . . when we remembered Zion. There on the poplars we hung our harps" (Psalm 137:1-2).

Paul and Silas can sing in prison. Habakkuk can stand steady as the Babylonians come over the horizon. But, you might say, "I am neither of the above or none of the above. When my world is rocked, I don't roll. I go down. The psalmist and I have much more in common than these others."

The captive couldn't sing for his captors. His prison wasn't one with bars, but life hemmed him in on every side, in every way. His captors had even imprisoned his emotions, beaten him down, silenced his songs. You sometimes see this in the faces of people around you. The person stands silent in the times of worship because instead of a song, he has a complaint, a question, a multitude of questions. "Why, God?" "How long, God?" "What do I do now, God?" The cell door is closed and the light is dim, the walls of emotion totally obscuring hope.

Wow. Welcome to the low point. The good news is that once you've descended to this level, the only direction you can head is up. It's like those times you found yourself at the bottom of the pool but then realized that you'd soon be out of breath. So what did you do? You planted both feet and pushed. Your lungs felt the pain of a lack of air, as if they were beginning to collapse in your chest like a deflating balloon. With your head bent back, eyes unable to focus because of the water but with the light above the surface clearly in view, you kicked and swam upward with all your strength. Then you hit the surface, gasping as your lungs filled with air. And it took a moment to convince yourself that everything was okay.

This passage of Scripture is like that, leaving us with the feeling that we're caught somewhere between the bottom of the pool and the top, where we can find the air we desperately need. The impact of this psalm leaves our brain dazed, and then the drowning feeling begins. "I'm not like Paul and Silas—I can't sing in prison. I'm not like Habakkuk—my faith can't rise above the circumstances. I'm like this guy. Just find me a tree and I'll hang up my harp."

Do that and you'll miss the point.

The point is: God is good. His goodness doesn't stop when we have difficulties. He's good in the hammock times and the hard times. The problem isn't the goodness of God. The problem is our failure to understand that His goodness isn't based on the goodness of our situations. When we index His goodness to our comfort then we rob ourselves of the greatest asset we have for those hard times: the goodness of God. At that point, we may not be able to see God's goodness in our situations. But like Paul and Silas we can keep our focus on God. Like Habakkuk, we can live by faith.

Fine statements. Typical sentiments. But how do you do that?

You Can Sing If You Remember the Words

HERE'S THE NEXT step. It's a step because it requires what we've already learned to be in place before we take it—the focus of Paul and Silas on God so they can sing, the faith of Habakkuk that the righteous will live by their faith.

Then add the next step: remember.

What did the psalmist say? "By the rivers of Babylon we sat and wept when we *remembered* Zion" (verse 1, emphasis added). The Tigris and Euphrates reminded them of home in a backhanded way. "Because I am here, I am not there." To stand by these rivers confronted the musician with reality—he was a captive, a prisoner, a slave in a pagan and idolatrous land. No longer was he surrounded by the people of God, but by an evil nation.

What else did the psalmist say? "If I forget you, O Jerusalem, may my right hand forget its skill. May my tongue cling to the roof of my mouth if I do not remember you, if I do not consider Jerusalem my highest joy" (verses 5-6). He knows it's so important to remember that he's even willing to forsake his talents to do so.

It's like an oath. If he forgets Jerusalem, may he also forget how to play the harp. If he forgets Jerusalem, may his tongue be paralyzed so that he can no longer speak or sing. This is an oath of devastating consequences. To forget would be to lose not just his music, but his hope, even his worship of the God he loves and serves.

He vows not only to remember a city, but all that it stood for and represented: the temple which now lay in ruins, the godly people who'd worshiped and served there, the Davidic throne that now seemed empty and not eternal, the Holy City where the pilgrims had come. His tears were bitter but determined—determined not to forget what should be his "highest joy."

Keep moving it up. Move from a city, to the place of the temple, to God Himself. Ramp it up to the level of the psalmist's worship. He didn't worship the stones and structures, but the God who inspired their construction. He'd played notes and sung words to God.

Not this day though. But something is going on, perhaps the almost imperceptible stirring of hope in his soul.

His harp is hung up. Hung. James Montgomery Boice thought this was significant. These exiles, "did not break their harps in pieces or throw them in the stream. Instead they hung them on the poplars, presumably saving them for what would surely be a better day."[4] Now start to look for the hope in this psalm, subtle but certain in the psalmist's action, words, and praying.

He finally expresses his determination not to let distress become an ultimate despair with a turn of phrase. "We sat and wept," he writes. "We hung our harps." And now his vow isn't of the crowd but of himself: "If I forget you . . . may my right hand forget its skill . . . my tongue cling to the roof of my mouth . . . if I do not remember you, if I do not consider Jerusalem my highest joy." He has a glimmer of hope, seemingly hidden but still hope, in these words. He doesn't destroy his harp, he doesn't allow the crowd to determine how he feels. Instead, the psalmist does the one thing that he can right then: he remembers.

Some do struggle with the remainder of the psalm. It's imprecatory in nature, calling on God to remember what had been done and to deal with those who did it. This man cries out his hurt to God and appeals for God to act according to His Word. Better to turn justice over to God than to harbor bitterness in one's heart. But don't get sidetracked and miss the point—the next step, the importance of remembering.

The Importance of Remembering

THE PSALMIST REMEMBERED. He kept alive the only ember that he could fan into flame. He kept it alive by remembering. In our downtimes, we can't forget.

Tom eventually remembered. In particular, he remembered verses that gave him confidence in the Lord's help. He remembered that God was in control of his life. In spite of his own attempts to end his life, God demonstrated that Tom's days were indeed in His hands. His family and his church were visible and tangible reminders of God's faithfulness and love. They didn't let him forget.

Depression is like a cruel jailer, enthusiastically doing his job, keeping the cell door closed. He confines the prisoner and blots out hope so that the past is more torment than encouragement. But when the past is a reminder of the faithfulness and love of God, the cell key begins to turn, hope renews, and the door opens.

Later, Tom would quote Lamentations 3:21-24, which begins with these words: "This I call to mind and therefore I have hope." What he remembered is this truth, "Because of the LORD's great love we are not consumed, for his compassions never fail. They are new every morning; great is your faithfulness."

In the silence of all that you face
God will give you His mercy and grace
Jesus never said
It was an easy road to travel
He only said that you would never be alone
So when your last thread of hope
Begins to come unraveled
Don't give up
He walks beside you
On this journey home and He knows

Life is hard, the world is cold
We're barely young and then we're old
But every falling tear is always understood
Yes, life is hard, but God is good.[5]

The truths that need to swarm around us to help us break out of the things imprisoning us include remembering. Perhaps you need to keep a journal, writing in it God's blessings. Or maybe you need to return to some special place to remind you how God worked in your life there, how someone ministered to you. Or it could be that reminders surround you, perhaps overlooked— maybe a well-worn Bible that you need to open once again.

Go back to the bottom of the pool, plant both feet, and push. Look up as you ascend toward the surface, eyes wide open, seeing the light, heading toward the air you so desperately need and want.

That's what remembering does. It pushes you back to the place where you can again sing the songs, where the praise can flow.

Study Guide

Part 1 — Getting into the Word

Prayer: Perhaps you've never looked at Psalm 137 this way, but now it makes sense. You can get so captured by your circumstances that you forget that God is good. Ask God to help you remember. Then pause in your praying, even if you're doing this study as a group. Allow for moments of silence, no matter how awkward they might feel. Then praise God for the blessings He brings to your mind.

Reading and Hearing God's Word: Read Psalm 137 and note the words that describe the psalmist's pain. The opening verses remind us that it's not always easy to sing, but also show the importance of remembering the good things of God.

Understanding God's Word: Read the psalm again and look for words and phrases that emphasize remembering. Underline or highlight these or make a list of them. What does the psalmist want God to remember?

Meditating on God's Word: Focus your attention on Psalm 137:5-6. This is a very severe prayer, asking God to deal with the person praying it! How does the intensity of the writer's determination to remember compare to your own?

Part 2 — Taking the Word into My World

You have learned about the psalmist's world and how this truth helped him. Now what about your world? To help you bring this truth into your situations, answer the following questions. They will help you take the truth of then and make it real in the time of now.

1. In worship, you respond to God, to all that He is and says and does. The psalmist is struggling in the opening verses. What is he responding to?

2. Difficulties will either drive a person away from God or nearer to God. At first, the difficulties seem to be driving the psalmist away. What makes the difference in his life?
3. Whether you are in a time of difficulty or not, list blessings of God, about God, and by God that you're determined to remember.

Part 3 — Grabbing Hold

It wasn't unusual for God to tell His people to build an altar so they'd remember a particular event. At times the patriarchs did it without being prompted. So here's a unique challenge: An old gospel song proclaims, "Here I raise my Ebenezer, hither by Thy help I've come." Find the Old Testament passage these words are from, read it, and then ask God to help you always remember His blessings.

And now a test! The vital truths learned so far are:

Chapter 1: _____

Chapter 2: _____

Chapter 3: _____

LIGHT FOR DARK DAYS — PRAY

PSALM 13

O ur locations had changed. No longer was I the pastor of the church he attended and neither of us still lived in the same city. Tim and his family had moved to Virginia while my family and I had relocated to a new place of ministry in Nebraska. E-mail kept us in contact — and one of his notes to me concluded with these words:

P.S. Megan starts kindergarten in three weeks!

The closing words of his e-mail brought a whirlwind of emotion and a rush of memories to mind, ones that began with the sound of the doorbell. There on our porch was a group of students from a nearby Bible college, out caroling — but now the songs of Christmas were the furthest thing from their minds. It had seemed like a fun thing to do after the college's Christmas banquet for faculty, staff, and students. Go visit some professors' homes and those of other friends they'd made at church and in the community, sing some songs of the season, wish them a merry Christmas, and head off to the next stop on the impromptu itinerary. Now the group stood in a panic at the door of the pastor's house.

"We saw an ambulance at Tim and Leanne's," were their first words. Whatever else they said, I missed most of it. Tim worked in the financial aid office at the school. Many students knew him and he attended the same church as most of the students in this group.

It was Tim and Leanne's first pregnancy. They were experiencing all the excitement of a baby on the way, to be born sometime in the late winter. They needed to ready the baby's room and secure a vast array of necessary items. Some would come by way of gifts and at showers, while they'd find others at garage sales, department stores, and on loan from friends. Each item was a small piece of a dream, a picture that would be incomplete until the day came when they would carry the precious addition to their family into their home and carefully lay her in the crib.

The ambulance was gone by the time I got to their street. Their neighbors were still awake, because the group of students had just recently left there. So in the days when cell phones were in their infancy, I needed to go somewhere to call the hospitals in the area, and theirs was the closest phone. They anxiously stood by as I dialed. A few phone calls later I dashed out of their kitchen, headed to the hospital where the ambulance had gone, still unsure of what occurred to prompt a 9-1-1 call.

Things had progressed well with the pregnancy until the fifth month. Nothing major, but something to watch. That December night, hemorrhaging began—much more than the spotting that sometimes occurred—and they quickly called the ambulance. The staff at the hospital didn't hesitate. The doctor quickly found Megan's faint heartbeat, then wheeled Leanne into the adjoining operating room. The doctor called for "crash anesthetic" and they performed an emergency C-section. Within four minutes after arriving at the hospital Megan came into the world, weighing all of 1 pound, 9.5 ounces. The pregnancy was only in its twenty-fifth week. Then the staff separated mother and child, one headed to the recovery room for careful monitoring as the anesthetic wore off, the other to the neonatal intensive care unit for monitoring of a different sort: one intended to sustain life, a fragile life.

The young couple who'd so carefully been planning for their

child's birth—preparing crib, blanket, pajamas, room, toys, and a special rocking chair for mother and child—began to experience what had never entered their minds. Their daughter's first crib would be sterile, with clear plastic sides, an opening to accommodate the attentions and examinations of a medical staff, with wheels for mobility and the ability to attach the things necessary to preserve life. Instead of a colorful mobile, over her were monitors, a ventilator, IVs, and feeding tubes. Her first blanket was hospital issued, her first pajamas a hospital gown, her first room a crowded sea of cribs with an ever-changing array of people.

All the expectations of having a baby had been dumped out and replaced by a scene that initially was one of horror. The image of mother and father with newborn child became one of medical technology, terminology, and hospital routine. Instead of a short walk down the hall to peer into her crib, it was many trips to the hospital, into the parking garage, up the elevator to the fourth floor, down the hall, turn left, left again, and then right. Scrub hands, arms, dress in hospital gowns, and finally a glance at the monitors that became so familiar. This isn't how they imagined it would be. A nursery is one thing, a neonatal intensive care unit quite another. But that's where Megan lived the early weeks of her life, and her parents faced that routine day by day for three full months.

Listen to her father's words: "As my wife and I made daily trips to the neonatal intensive care unit, our stomachs would tighten in anticipation of the scene that was waiting for us. Would Megan be having a good day or a bad one? Or worse, would this be her last day? And again, our thoughts would drift to 'Why would God put this in our lives?' Ultimately, I believe the questions came from fright, feeling helpless—maybe even a bit of guilt, thinking maybe we had done something to deserve this situation. These thoughts led to a feeling of chaos in our lives, way beyond what we thought we were capable of handling."

Those were dark days.

The Expression of Despair

YOU MIGHT BE wondering, "When is this book going to encourage me? It seems to pick me up a bit, but then it knocks me lower." Understand that light is best appreciated in the dark. It's been said that the most important light in the house isn't the beautiful chandelier in the front hallway, but the bare bulb that lights the back steps in the middle of the night. When it's dark, we know we need light—and we squint for every glimmer. Perhaps that's why God gives us so many dark scenes, difficult times, people whose lives experience trouble. Just like us, people in the Bible had dark days when they needed light, and we learn from them.

And God gives light.

There are 150 psalms in the book of Psalms and only one of them has no hope. That's Psalm 88. Read it, but don't stop with the last verse. Read on to the opening verse of the next psalm. There's a purpose in the placing of these two psalms next to each other. Psalm 89 ends Book III and Psalm 90 begins the next major section of the Psalms. Psalms 88 and 89 are bumped up next to each other, bringing to an end, preparing for a beginning. Some think they should be read together, especially because both are *maskils*: teaching psalms with lessons for us to learn.

We read Psalm 88, and there's no hope. The last words are "the darkness is my closest friend." What we need is light for dark days, so we keep reading. The next verse (Psalm 89:1) says, "I will sing of the LORD's great love forever." Singing again! Hope lives! In the one psalm we are called to a higher kind of faith, a faith that says "I'm going to trust God even when it looks like I'm as good as dead." Then the next psalmist stands to read what he has written, and he writes of singing, not of the intense despairing struggle of the previous psalmist's soul—of light, not darkness. And our hearts realize that God is telling us about the light we need in the dark days.

Still, there are days when our hearts' hurts are best summed up by the words of David in Psalm 13:

How long, O Lord? Will you forget me forever?
How long will you hide your face from me?
How long must I wrestle with my thoughts and every day
have sorrow in my heart?
How long will my enemy triumph over me? (Psalm 13:1-2)

These verses are an expression of despair. As you read them you find the extent of the writer's anguish as four times he asks, "How long?" The intensity of David's emotions is obvious, reflecting the agony of his soul because it looked like his situation would go on and on and on. These could have been Tim and Leanne's words: "How long?" Doctors gave their guesses but only God knew for sure how long it would be before they could take their daughter home—or if they ever would. These words may be yours at times.

The psalmist felt alienated from God. He reached out for that comforting presence, but like a new widow—who finds an emptiness where once a loving spouse had been—he felt as if God wasn't there. He'd always been there, but it didn't feel that way now.

David has troubled thoughts, a hurting heart, and he's looking to God for an answer to his question of "How long?" Can you relate to that? We also have troubled thoughts and hurting hearts, and it's as if we look to God and say the same words he did: "God, how long is this going to go on?"

David knows the cause of his despair: it's in his thoughts and it's the sorrow in his heart. He knows, yet he doesn't. He just knows the feeling is there. He doesn't really have all the answers because the questions aren't all that clear. All he knows is that he doesn't know. Remember Tim's words: "fright, feeling helpless, and maybe even a bit of guilt." They fit here all too well. The psalmist knows that his thoughts trouble him, that he has sorrow in his heart, that he faces an unnamed enemy. It's not God's fault, but God isn't fixing it either, and he feels completely forgotten.

It may well be that David wrote this psalm during the time when Saul had turned against him. The king he'd served, stayed loyal to—the Lord's anointed whom he would not lift his own hand against—hunted him like a predator going after its prey. And it just doesn't seem to end. David wishes Saul would forget him in the same way he feels that God has. If only he could hide as well as it seems God has hidden His face. The wrestling match going on in his mind seems to never end, every day adding more sorrow to the sorrows already stored in his heart. His emotions are restless as is his life itself—ever moving, always on the go, staying at least one step ahead of the pursuit.

The Expression of Prayer

THE FIRST TWO verses of Psalm 13 are complaint and the next two are petition, pure and simple. God gives us this psalm and in our darkness gives us light. And we learn from David yet another step. Paul and Silas sing, Habakkuk has faith, and we're on our way. Remember the next first step, the one from Psalm 137? It was just that: *remember.* The harp may be hanging on the tree but we must never forget. We must always remember. Now in the darkness, God gives light—and we see it in David's praying. No sugar-coated, rote-learned, habit-repeated, pious-toned performance. Just the cry of a man who sees death and pleads for life.

> *Look on me and answer, O LORD my God.*
> *Give light to my eyes, or I will sleep in death;*
> *My enemy will say, "I have overcome him,"*
> *and my foes will rejoice when I fall. (verses 3-4)*

"Let me see! Give light to my eyes!" David cries. His complaint has given way to petition—and that's what we need to do. We need help, understanding, and strength, so we cry out to God. Even in those difficult times, the truth remains that God is good, all the time—but it's as if the truth is obscured, cloudy, unapparent in the dark times.

For David, the times were so dark that death appeared imminent, as imminent as that spear impulsively thrown across the room by King Saul, the one to whom he continued to show loyalty. David had killed Goliath, attained a high rank in the army, and pleased the people. They danced and sang, "Saul has slain his thousands, and David his tens of thousands" (1 Samuel 18:7). Then the jealous king grabs a weapon and hurls it, saying, "I'll pin David to the wall" (18:11). Twice David eluded him.

And death appeared as imminent as realizing that the one pursuing him through the wilderness regions has unwittingly chosen the same cave, closing off all avenues of escape, trapping him against the impenetrable walls of rock. Trapped! The light at the cave's entrance silhouettes the figure of the man who more than anyone else in the world wants him dead. Yet David chose not to enter a prison of his own doing, an action that could have haunted him. Instead there at En Gedi he refused to lift his hand against the king, "for he is the anointed of the LORD" (1 Samuel 24:6).

At times his refuge was among his enemies, those who should have delighted in his capture and execution—they became his safe haven. Those he'd fought against became the ones who helped him elude his adversary. The slayer of the champion of the Philistines took his men and settled in Gath, serving King Achish for nearly a year and a half. The walls of that city did allow him to come and go. No jailer prevented him but he was confined—and his alone hours were like solitary confinement, no one to cry out to but God.

David the anointed one, the most hunted one. The hero was now a wanted man—it just didn't make sense.

Yet the subtle but certain truth remains: God is good and His goodness is active. It's not passive, not unmoved. His goodness is as close as a whispered prayer. The evidence? David is alive in spite of the state-instituted, supported, and energized "dead-or-alive" (preferably dead) manhunt. God has anointed David king and nothing will thwart His plan. All the efforts of the most powerful man in the country can't accomplish more than God will allow.

And in His infinite goodness, God hears prayer. In this psalm we transition from the expression of despair to David's expression of prayer. It's a threefold petition, a prayer of urgency, spurred by the realization that his life is in danger and his defeat a possibility.

Sometimes God allows crises knowing that even His faithful people will respond with increased praying. Just as the events of September 11, 2001, spurred the patriotism of our land, adversities and difficulties drive us to pray. And yes, it's exactly what needs to happen. We need to pray. Yes, Paul and Silas sang, but they also prayed. Yes, Habakkuk learned that the righteous will live by their faith, but he learned it as he took his complaints to God, praying. The temple musician hung up his harp, exchanging his praises for pleadings, praying for God to intervene. Slowly we begin to see a pattern, a response, a reachable foothold to help us in hard times. And underneath it all is the goodness of God, just as real and reliable but even more desired than ever.

"Look!"

"Look!" David cries, "Look on me!" It felt as though God was looking the other direction. We get frustrated with other people when we need and don't get their attention. "Would you at least just take a look at this proposal?" we might say to our boss. "Could you look into this situation and see if there is something that can be done here?" We know nothing will happen unless the right person sees. "Sees." That's at the heart of it. If it's brought to their attention, catches their eye, then something will be done.

"Look!" David is saying, "God, do you see what's going on in my life?"

And sometimes we say the same thing, as if God isn't looking our way, that maybe He's unaware of what's happening. Do you really think God never knows what's going on in your life? The answer to that question ought to "scare you spitless," as I like to say, because God *does* know what's going on in your life. All the time! We may enjoy the answer/response "God is good—all the time." But perhaps we need one that says, "God knows—all the time." He does know, which should scare us, in a sense, because He knows our failings and fallings. More importantly, it should comfort us.

Why should this comfort us? When we're going through the hard times—those times when it seems like God is silent or even sleeping, when it seems that God is looking the other way—remember, God knows. The problem isn't with God keeping track of us, but with us staying on track with God. We're the wanderers, not God. Our vision is nearsighted and shortsighted, not His. We can handle only so many pieces of information, limited in our ability to multitask. But His capacity is infinite; we'll never be lost in the cracks.

"Answer!"

And like David we ask God to answer. We want answers, sooner rather than later. Now would be good! Tim and Leanne asked for answers. Remember their question? "Why would God put this in our lives?" David wanted to be freed from his despair. He needed answers to his questions. That's the way we think. "If I only knew . . . " But if we did know what was ahead, we'd probably despair even more! We'd probably find ourselves arguing with God, judging His plans to be inadequate from our selfish point of view. If we did know, it would weaken our faith because we'd have no need for faith if the outcomes were already revealed. Still we ask.

"Give Light!"

The next part of David's petition is part new petition and part repetition. The Hebrew poets would sometimes say the same thing more than once, adding new words or phrases, adjusting the perspective, intensifying the insights. "Look; answer; give light," David prayed. Really not much difference. He wants to know he has God's attention. He wants God to answer him, to free him from his confusion and despair. And he says, "Give me light," because in those dark days—in those times when everything looked so hopeless—David needed to be able to see.

There's urgency in this prayer, a threefold expression of urgency because David realizes that if something doesn't change, the end will be death. Perhaps in his heart his prayer felt like this: "I'm going down, and I don't think I can ever get up again. If I go down any more I'm down for good, God. Unless You give me light, unless You look my way, unless You answer me, my enemy will overcome me and my foes will rejoice."

When those dark days come, we need light. And there it was. So near and yet so far, so familiar and yet so often unrecognized. Hidden in the open. We've said it repeatedly but failed to hear it even once. David is showing us yet we can be too slow to catch it. In the middle of all that's going wrong, when the light of life itself is in danger of being snuffed out, David prays, knowing that God is the One he must turn to, the One he must trust.

The Expression of Praise

Our focus is on the troubles, David's on his trust. In *God* he trusts:

> But I trust in your unfailing love;
> my heart rejoices in your salvation.
> I will sing to the LORD,
> for he has been good to me. (Psalm 13:5-6)

Before, David has been saying, "Look on me and answer. . . . Give light to my eyes," but now he's saying, "I will sing." Out of the darkness a song, a raised voice, words flowing. What's changed? Nothing. There's no indication of a sudden victory, a change of heart by his pursuer, or a withdrawal of enemy troops. The situation is still the same!

Before he's saying, "Give me light," and "Look; answer me." Now he says, "Let me sing." But there's no indication at this point that all the trouble is gone. There's no indication that the depression is totally removed. But in the darkness that remains he says, "I will trust." His monologue with God stays just that, a one-sided discussion. But it concludes where it must, with trust.

He expresses calm confidence, based on the truth that is settled in his heart—God's faithfulness, His unfailing love—the *hesed* of God. Now we start to get a firm grasp on why we can say at all times that "God is good—all the time." Because God's love is unfailing. David prays to the faithful God.

Prayers can be perfunctory, recitations, forms followed to fill the time allotment. Or prayers can be the cry of the soul, grasping the throne of heaven, pleading for God to work. David's prayer is an example of the latter. While some people are content to leave praying for others to do, David wasn't. If praying helps you see the goodness of God and to experience the reality of His faithfulness, it must be your own praying, your own pleading, you on your face before God.

Night can be the most difficult time. You lie down but can't sleep, or you fall asleep but wake and stare at the clock. Your mind won't let you rest. So use the time, use these truths. Perhaps right then you need to turn your thoughts to praise, to have faith, to remember, to pray. These are steps that help you break out of the thoughts and things that swarm and surround you and instead remind you that God is good.

Tim and Leanne later wrote, "We believe we were able to find God's peace when we began to look outside our emotion and reach for something we knew was stable, unmoving: God's being, His promises, and His goodness. While God's promises didn't seem to make the situation 'all better,' He provided a way for us to deal with our circumstances." They had to trust Him.

One evening as they were taking a break during their time at the hospital visiting Megan, they began to ask each other why God had allowed this to happen. They also talked openly about what they would do if Megan didn't survive. Here are their words: "As we faced this potential reality, we had nothing left to hold onto but God's sovereignty. We had to believe that if that was His plan— though we couldn't imagine facing it—God was in complete control and would walk beside us every step of the way. It wasn't a question of 'Was God going to be good to us by allowing Megan to live?' but rather, 'How was God going to demonstrate His goodness to us?' God's goodness wouldn't hinge upon our happiness and desires, but would be done regardless in accomplishing His own perfect plan."

And now they know a piece of that plan: "P.S. Megan starts kindergarten in three weeks!"

Study Guide

Part 1 — Getting into the Word

Prayer: Do you need to pray what David prayed? The parallels between the cry of his heart and your cry can be striking. Your situation may not be the same as David's, but the sentiment is. Words written centuries ago still resonate with meaning today because God's eternal Word speaks to all people of all times. Pray that God will use this prayer in your life today.

Reading and Hearing God's Word: Read Psalm 13 aloud. Then read it again, with feeling. Imagine how David might have said these words. Try to make the verses sound like they are your words addressed to God. Verse 5 mentions God's "unfailing love." It may take some effort, but try to find some other verses that mention this phrase and write a definition of what it means.

Understanding God's Word: Read the psalm again. Underline any key phrases or ideas. Then answer the following questions:

1. What was going on in David's life when he wrote this psalm?
2. Explain in your own words each of his petitions.
   a. "Look"
   b. "Answer"
   c. "Give light"
3. Describe how your life would be affected by the answer to that prayer.
4. David trusted in God's unfailing love. Explain what it means to trust.

Meditating on God's Word: Now write a paragraph telling how you trust in God's unfailing love. If you're doing this as a group study, share what you wrote with others.

Part 2 — Taking the Word into My World

People are quickest to pray in times of trouble. When things are going well or are "even keeled," it's easy to neglect prayer. Then there are times when people trust their own abilities to get through a situation rather than relying on God. So with that in mind,

1. How would you describe your life right now?
2. If your prayer life were on the table would it need surgery because it's sick, an autopsy to figure out why it died, or could it be a teaching model to encourage others to pray?
3. If you have a special need, write a prayer to God and begin the first part with the phrase "Look on me," the next with the word "Answer," and the final section with "Give light." Make it real, relevant, and personal.

Part 3 — Grabbing Hold

Sometimes we're better at padding the pew than bending the knee. Perhaps the best conclusion to this study is to spend time on your knees. Commit to being a person who prays, not only in times of despair but in all times. Pray until you can praise.

ON THICK ICE — TRUST

LAMENTATIONS 3:22-23

If we lived life always expecting something unexpected, then perhaps we'd never be surprised. But as an old saying goes, "Life is full of surprises." Situations change, plans alter, hopes go unfulfilled. Then we realize our confidence in the future puts us into a prison of our own making. The door clangs shut unexpectedly. And the unexpected becomes a personal corrections officer, holding us in a new place of emotional confinement.

It happens. And it happened to Ed and June. While this couple had undoubtedly seen many of the varied colors of life, one thing was steady and on track: Ed was closing in on retirement.

He was just in his late thirties when a pharmaceutical company hired him as a salesman. It remained his place of employment for the next twenty-plus years. Age happens, retirement approaches, plans are made. Hope begins to loom large. He and his wife made plans for the future, plans to live the rest of their lives in Yuba City, California. And everything seemed to be on track.

During his years with the company, Ed had noticed that no other salesmen ever received full retirement. But he determined that he'd be the first. It became his goal, motivator, and energizer to keep him moving forward. The hours he put in and the effort he made seemed to be paying off. He maintained his position as one of the top salesmen in the district. Twenty-one years down, seven to go.

What could go wrong? He was a longtime employee, loyal, hardworking, not coasting to retirement, focused to finish strong, a committed follower of God. And he prayed that God would grant him what no other salesman achieved. The picture of the future was enviable, one filled with scenes of familiar surroundings, adequate income, enjoyment of the things that couples not hindered by job responsibilities could enjoy.

Ed was fifty-nine, with less than six years to go when he was asked to take early retirement. It was unexpected. Everything he was working to avoid became reality. His focus had been so clear, so directed, so specific—and now it was so hard to give up. Sometimes the shock of the unexpected paralyzes our brains and plants a seed of anticipation. Unfortunately, this isn't some positive anticipation, but a worry of when the other shoe will drop. For a year, Ed and June waited for that to happen, living shortsighted, not remembering that God was still good—far more than they could possibly realize. They were caged in, unable to break out, jailed by the turn of events that they'd tried so carefully to avoid but which had become unmistakable reality.

The other shoe turned out to be a decision they made themselves, led by God. Ed decided that he needed to return to school, to get further training, to prepare himself for a career that would last only a few years. His love for the Lord and God's Word were at the center of his decision to attend seminary. Perhaps with a master's degree in Bible he could teach at a small Bible college. For the first time in the thirty-eight years of their married life, June faced working outside the home as the self-appointed minimum-wage breadwinner while her sixty-year-old hubby attended school. Their step of obedience to the Lord's leading put them in the place where they could learn to trust God's faithfulness.

And they did see His faithfulness! After three months, they decided that June should give two-weeks' notice at her job in the school's mailroom and return to being the full-time keeper of their home. When she told her supervisor that her husband wanted her to stay at home and that he planned to find a job, her boss asked,

"Has he ever put his resumé in here at the school?" He did just that and was hired to work in the development department. His people skills as an experienced salesman were greatly used. He earned more money in his position than she had in the mailroom, plus they no longer had to pay tuition costs. Unknown to them when he applied for the position, students who worked at the school didn't pay tuition.

God even gave them a new direction. Ed did earn his master's degree, but he didn't become a teacher. Instead he stayed in stewardship work. What he did first for the college, he then did for the Back to the Bible ministry in Lincoln, Nebraska. Then, at age sixty-seven, God called him home. He spent his last seven years on earth serving the Lord in full-time ministry, and learning of God's faithfulness and goodness step by step. God taught Ed and June the importance of trusting Him in difficult times.

Great Is His Faithfulness

PERHAPS IT'S HARD for you to say "Great is His faithfulness" without thinking about the great hymn introduced in 1954 at a Billy Graham crusade in England. What was then a new song wasn't the result of a particular dramatic experience, but simply of the author's morning-by-morning realization of God's faithfulness. Perhaps the songwriter's financial situation had made him more keenly aware that God proved Himself faithful daily. His health had been poor, and he was forced to resign from the ministry. Thomas Chisholm wrote, "My income has not been large at any time due to impaired health in the earlier years which has followed me until now, although I must not fail to record the unfailing faithfulness of a covenant-keeping God, for which I am filled with astonishing gratefulness."[1]

The theme of that song, God's faithfulness, was a truth known by Ed and June and, of course, by countless others. This truth is expressed succinctly in a somewhat unexpected place in the Bible. At first glance it may sound like a verse from the Psalms, perhaps one of the sections that resonates with praise, but it isn't. Instead, it's from the book of Lamentations, a collection of five funeral poems that commemorate the fall of Jerusalem to the Babylonians in 586 B.C. Annually, Orthodox Jews customarily read the entire book aloud on the traditional date of the destruction of the temple. Many read it weekly at the Western Wall of the Temple Mount, at what is called the Wailing Wall, in Jerusalem.

Many Bible scholars believe that Jeremiah wrote Lamentations at a time of sorrow and ruin, when people's hearts were failing them for fear, and people in turn were failing each other. Jeremiah was probably an eyewitness of the events remembered in these poems. He saw the destruction and shared the overwhelming sense of loss. The people of Israel saw their city, their temple, and even their rituals destroyed. And then their captors took them into exile.

God directed Jeremiah to record the horrors of this scene not just for historical preservation, but like the rest of Scripture, also for the lessons we need to learn from it. The apex of the book is in Lamentations 3, Jeremiah's response in the midst of his affliction—the point where he says, "Great is your faithfulness."

Learning to Trust God's Faithfulness

BUT DON'T JUST start reading at chapter three. If you do, you'll shortchange yourself, and miss out on the beauty, scope, and flow of this too often overlooked book of the Bible.

Often, our tendency with Scripture is to take the tastiest slices and leave the rest. For example, Romans 8 contains more than a single verse, yet we seem to be content with knowing only verse 28, "And we know that in all things God works for the good of those who love him, who have been called according to his purposes." In the same way, Lamentations contains much more than the phrase "great is your faithfulness." Set it in its context, understand it better, and use the truth contained in it to help you further along in your growth. That way, no matter what situation you find yourself in, you'll be able to say that God is good because you've learned to trust in His faithfulness.

Lamentations contains the words of a broken heart, its pages stained with the tears of the prophet Jeremiah. It's the only book in the Bible that is entirely laments. Its poems are for the funeral of the once-beautiful city of Jerusalem. As we read and reread these words, we keep alive the memory of that event and we learn how to deal with suffering.

Remembering God's faithfulness isn't reserved only for the good times. It's not something to be done only by those experiencing the good life. We're to remember God's goodness all the time, and this step is necessary if we're to truly comprehend His goodness. But you must do more than listen to the Word and you must even do more than learn what it teaches. You must *live* the Word, living out the truth of trusting God. You must live on the thick ice of trusting in God's faithfulness.

This must have been tough on Jeremiah, both the memory of these events and the events themselves.

Joshua's warning had become reality. Eight hundred years earlier, the leader of the nation had said,

But just as every good promise of the LORD your God has come true, so the LORD will bring on you all the evil he has threatened, until he has destroyed you from this good land he has given you. If you violate the covenant of the LORD your God, which he commanded you, and go and serve other gods and bow down to them, the LORD's anger will burn against you, and you will quickly perish from the good land he has given you. (Joshua 23:15-16)

For more than forty years, Jeremiah prophesied of the coming judgment. But the people rejected his preaching and scorned him. Then the city fell. A month later, the enemy burned the temple. Jeremiah witnessed the destruction of the city walls and the towers that represented its strength, the homes of the people, the palace of the king, and the temple of the Lord. His writing comes from his pain. The one known as the weeping prophet in these writings laments all the more with bitter suffering and heartbreak. Yet in the midst of sorrow and ruin, he remembers the mercy of the Lord! "His compassions never fail" (Lamentations 3:22). We may fail Him, but He cannot fail us.

What we can always have—should have—is hope. This is a hope based on God's faithfulness. It's a hope that thrives because we trust in God. Lamentations 1 and 5 focus attention on the people of Jerusalem who'd sinned and ultimately cried out to God to remember and restore. Lamentations 2 and 4 focus on the Lord, who deals with His people and their sins. Central in the structure is Lamentations 3, Jeremiah's response in the middle of the affliction of his people. And amazingly, he focuses on the goodness of God. Think about what he writes here! In his words you find a resource, a response to those who might say, "How can you say God is good even when times are bad?" There are three things in these verses that stand out. Each tell us how we can always say, "God is good."

He Is the Lord of Hope

The first is this: Trust in the hope God offers. Jeremiah says, "I remember my affliction and my wandering, the bitterness and the gall. I well remember them, and my soul is downcast within me. Yet this I call to mind and therefore I have hope" (Lamentations 3:19-21). The list of what he recalls begins with God's love that keeps us from being consumed, overwhelmed by our circumstances. It includes the ongoing, never failing compassion of God along with the fact that every single day, as surely as the sun rises in the morning, God's love and compassion are renewed. "Great is your faithfulness," he proclaims.

Nothing sugar-coated in these words. Instead Jeremiah uses the words *affliction, wandering, bitterness,* and *gall.* He tells of his downcast soul. Consider the list that leads to these words, the events that Jeremiah has gone through personally or witnessed:

(1) The siege of Jerusalem, (2) The famine in the city, (3) The flight of the army and the king, (4) The burning of the palace, temple, and city, (5) The breaching of the city walls, (6) The exile of the populace, (7) The looting of the temple, (8) The execution of the leaders, (9) The vassal status of Judah, and (10) The collapse of the expected foreign help.[2] And still, he has hope!

What would you put on a "Top Ten List" of reasons to be depressed, discouraged, and to have a downcast soul? (1) Downturn in the market in 2001, (2) WTC, (3) Anthrax, (4) Doctor's diagnosis, (5) Loss of a family member, (6) Downsized right out the door. . . . Some events could be on anyone's list or everyone's list. Others would just be on yours. The result would be concrete evidence to justify feeling like Jeremiah—ready to weep, fully prepared to write funeral poems. Jeremiah remembers, and so do you. He remembers these things well, and so do you. His soul is downcast, as perhaps is yours.

Yet he has hope. Do you?

To hope is to wait, to expect. Jeremiah has enough hope to wait. His expectation isn't based on economic forecasts, anticipated military actions, medical research, or grief counselors. His hope rests securely on God. His approach isn't an irrational response, an escaping from reality, or a misinterpretation of past events. No, he does remember but he's determined not to be controlled by the past. Instead, his focus is on God who is faithful. That's what he so purposefully "calls to mind" in the end. Forget and be downcast. Or "call to mind" and have hope.

With hope comes waiting. But the hope found here isn't a hope that says, "It's not now but maybe it will happen later"—a "hope-so" kind of hope. No. It's a hope that *knows*, that says, "I wait now and it *will* be later." Sometimes we hope for things in a way that sounds like we're wishing for something. Not so for Jeremiah. His was a "know-so" hope. He hoped because he knew.

The word *remember* has returned. A psalmist by the river in Babylon hangs up his harp and vows to never forget. Psalm 137, remember? Now the prophet Jeremiah shows the same mind-set.

He remembers. Perhaps we should pause and review, do something to remind us of the lessons being learned. Get out that 3x5 card again, or uncap the lipstick and head for the bathroom mirror to add more to what you wrote there before. You've written the earlier truths: (1) Sing, (2) Have faith, (3) Remember. Now add these: (4) Pray and (5) Trust!

Surround yourself with these! And the way to have hope is to trust the God who is faithful.

Do you want to be like Paul and Silas, who could sing in prison, like Habakkuk, who knew what it means to live by faith? Do you want to be like the temple musician who remembered and like David, who prayed? Then remember to hope in God, the God who is always faithful. And when you do, you'll have hope like Jeremiah—because we worship and serve the God of hope.

And Jeremiah is not finished yet either! It only gets better.

He Is the Lord of Love

Second, trust that God is the God of love. Leading up to Jeremiah's declaration of the faithfulness of God, he points out this truth: the love and mercy of God. "Because of the LORD's great love we are not consumed, for his compassions never fail" (Lamentations 3:22). Not only do these verses bring back the idea of remembering, but they also bring back thoughts of *hesed*, God's unfailing love. This word is used about 250 times in the Old Testament. It's not a narrow-spectrum word but a broadband term—comprehensive, and encompassing traits such as God's love, grace, mercy, goodness, forgiveness, truth, compassion, and faithfulness. "Great love," Jeremiah writes.

God's love is one that will not fail. It can't or He wouldn't be God. We live in a world of failing love. As a pastor, sometimes someone will say to me, "I don't love my wife anymore." He may have even reached the point of saying, "And I never loved her." I usually try to back him up a bit and say, "Now wait a minute. You *never* loved her?" The truth is, someone who says this has talked himself into the idea that he never loved his spouse. As his pastor, I'd remember the time I was with him in the hospital when their baby was born and saw both his and his wife's joy and love for each other, for their newly expanded family. Or I might remember the way they were there for each other in the hospital as one was going through surgery or at a time when the other had been rushed to the emergency room. I'd think about the experiences of life that I'd witnessed, scenes that gave evidence of love. All this is proof that "I never loved" are words of self-deception, a meager attempt to justify his failure to keep his marital commitment.

Sometimes people get even more confused and they think of God the way they think of others. But we can't think of God that way. People may fail us, but that will never happen in our relationship with God. God's love is a faithful love; God's love is an unfailing love; God's love will continue; God's love will be there. And sometimes in the worst of our situations, we look around and say, "Where's God's love?" God's love is still there. His love will not fail.

Great indeed is the *hesed* of God for us. Great enough that the word here is a plural, a Hebrew literary device that adds to its greatness. "Though he brings grief, he will show compassion, so great is his unfailing love" (Lamentations 3:32).

God will never suffer compassion fatigue. We do, but He doesn't. Our compassion receptors get worn down. The appeals come in the mail, tugging on our emotions with the close-ups of children in need. Refugees flood the border, fleeing the conflict and the approaching winter weather. Network news teams cover the growing tent cities, set up with humanitarian aid, in full color, beamed by satellite into our homes. Telephone solicitors call, asking for our support of their charity. Pictures of people in need are even placed by cash registers in convenience stores, with a can attached, for your loose change to help with their crises. And don't forget the telethons, charity concerts, and collection buckets with red crosses on them, passed through the stands at halftime. You probably can add to this list several more appeals, made many other ways. And which comes first: the empty wallet or the compassion fatigue? Often we run out of compassion first. Not so with God. His compassions never fail.

Imagine that it's your turn to be in need. Perhaps your house has been destroyed by fire or your child needs treatment that goes well beyond the coverage limits of your insurance. Suddenly, the bake sale outside the supermarket is for you. Now you're the one making the appeal. But compassion-exhausted people look the other way to avoid making eye contact, and quicken their paces as they try to shuffle past, hoping they don't have to say no to your face. While we may learn the hard way that people turn away, remember that God never does. His compassions never fail because of His *hesed,* His unfailing love.

Tonight you go to bed. Tomorrow will come. The sun rises every day and sets every day. Every day. And every morning there is light once again, a reminder that the Lord's compassions never fail—they *are* new every morning. And because of His love and compassion, we are not consumed.

Life can be overwhelming. It certainly was for Jeremiah. Go back to the "Top Ten List" of his day. That was more than enough to bury a person emotionally and spiritually, and it affected him physically as well. Now pull out your list, the one made for your time, your situation, your miseries. God is good, even in the worst of times. No matter how helpless and hopeless things may appear, He will not allow you to be consumed because of His love.

He Is the Lord of Faithfulness

THIRD, TRUST IN God's faithfulness. Jeremiah states what has become so familiar, the words that became the great hymn "Great Is Thy Faithfulness." Warren Wiersbe writes, "Here at the heart of this book we find one of the greatest confessions of faith found anywhere in the Bible."[3] We read here again of God's faithful love for His unfaithful people.

No thin ice here. One time in northern Minnesota—where the temperatures are among the coldest in the U.S. and where people even build homes with heat in the floors of their garages—near International Falls, the self-proclaimed "Icebox of the United States," the person who picked me up at the airport said, "When we go ice fishing, we have to put extensions on our augers because the ice is four feet deep." So they just drive out on the ice, set up houses, drill their holes, and fish.

If you've never driven a fully loaded conversion van onto a frozen lake you're probably shuddering at the thought. "Lakes are for driving *by*, not driving *on*!" My friends in Minnesota will chuckle at the thought that people would be afraid to ride out onto the lake. They understand the difference between thin ice and thick ice.

Nothing about the faithfulness of God is like thin ice. His faithfulness is characterized by firmness, fidelity, and certainty. God never cheats on us; God never gives up on us. His love for us is steadfast.

When He wanted to illustrate it in the most powerful way He could, God told the prophet Hosea to go out and marry a whore. As she continued in her ways of immorality, Hosea demonstrated a faithfulness of love for her, his unfaithful wife. He became a living metaphor, an example of God's love for us. God describes our unfaithfulness as spiritual adultery. He uses that powerful image to say to us, "When you walk away from Me, you're like a person committing adultery, cheating on his or her spouse. You're like the whore that Hosea married."

That's a strong image, isn't it? But it clearly describes things the way they really are — that the spiritual wanderer is cheating on God. Yet, God is still going to love us faithfully. He said in Hosea 2:19, "I will betroth you to me forever; I will betroth you in righteousness and justice, in love and compassion." That's God's faithful love for His unfaithful people. When Jeremiah looked toward God, he saw faithfulness.

He Is the Lord of Salvation
Fourth, trust in His salvation.

> *I say to myself, "The LORD is my portion;*
> *therefore I will wait for him."*
> *The LORD is good to those whose hope is in him,*
> *to the one who seeks him;*

it is good to wait quietly
for the salvation of the LORD. (Lamentations 3:24-26)

God saves us. Salvation speaks of His rescue and the resulting safety we can know. Notice carefully the phrase "it is good to wait quietly for . . . " Put the emphasis on "good to wait." Salvation isn't something we do; it's what God does. Salvation isn't something we accomplish; salvation is what we receive.

Think of salvation in terms of your decision to become a follower of Christ. God planned that. He provided for your salvation through the blood of Jesus, who died, was buried, and rose again. As a pledge of your inheritance, He gave you the Holy Spirit. That's all straight out of Ephesians 1. And it's all the work of God. We're saved not by anything we do, but by faith—a faith in the grace of God that reaches out to us. Our only part is an act of surrender to His work and His Lordship.

Now think of salvation in terms of the tough times of life. We may have exhausted our resources, emptied our bank accounts, pursued all possible medical options, worked hard and long—and yet we still need rescue. God will rescue us. The only question is "When?"

This is tough to say but very necessary. Complete healing may come only when we enter the presence of God. But once we do, the past with its pain will be gone. The situation that seems to never end one day will. Perhaps within our earthly lifetimes, perhaps not. But the goodness of God *will* ultimately correct all the wrongs. You can count on it.

This isn't an easy lesson to learn, but it's an important one. Jeremiah indicates this when he writes, "It is good for a man to bear the yoke while he is young" (Lamentations 3:27). Some might think he's saying that younger people can handle pain and stress better. That's not the case. Instead, his words point to the discipline that a person can learn from God—a kind of training that we can experience. By learning it in youth, it can benefit the greater portion of our lives. Some of the saddest words spoken are, "I wish I'd learned this a long time ago." Jeremiah is declaring the positive side of that—saying it's good to learn from God when we are young. What do we need to learn? That "the Lord is good to those whose hope is in him," and that "it is good to wait quietly for the salvation of the LORD."

Sometimes we must wait—and that's hard on people conditioned to microwave ovens, fast food, broadband Internet connections, instant everything. We want all the pain to go away now when what we need to do is trust in God's faithfulness. We need to trust His mysterious style of working on this planet, because whatever He does and however He does it will flow from His goodness.

Remember to trust in God's faithfulness. Because God is good.

Study Guide

Part 1 — Getting into the Word

Prayer: You've probably sung the hymn "Great Is Thy Faithfulness." Now ask God to help you grasp its meaning. It must be more than a piece of music if the truth of this passage will be used of God to help you in a time of difficulty.

Reading and Hearing God's Word: Read Lamentations 3:19-27. Better yet, read the entire book! It's not that long. Then you can focus on these verses. Perhaps you never noticed what leads into and out of the familiar part about God's faithfulness.

Understanding God's Word: Go over Lamentations 3:19-27 again carefully. Underline any key phrases or ideas. Then answer the following questions:

1. What are the key words that emphasize the prophet's distress?
2. In what way would you say that verse 21 is a turning point?
3. Define *hope* and show how verse 25 fits that definition. Does it sound like hope is something active, something you do, or is it totally passive?

4. How do you reconcile the emphasis on "seeking" in verse 25 and "waiting" in verse 26?

Meditating on God's Word: Write a brief summary of a meaningful verse or idea in this passage.

Part 2 — Taking the Word into My World

God didn't give us His Word just to increase our knowledge but to affect the way that we live. To make His truth real in our lives today involves applying the timeless truths of a passage such as this and making them timely truths for us today. Answer the following questions to help you see these verses as more than just the basis of a familiar hymn but as the help you can also cling to.

1. Jeremiah remembers the tough times. Read verses 19 and 20 again. If you were writing these verses, what would be the tough times you might remember?

2. Lamentations 3:21 sounds emphatic. Jeremiah makes a choice to think about something else. Rather than mull over the past pain, what does the prophet focus on?

3. The result is hope. What specifically, according to verses 22 to 24, should you focus on in order to have hope today? Make a list of everything you find in those verses and define each. Then try to come up with an example from your life.

Part 3 — Grabbing Hold

The saying may be well worn but still it holds true: "I may not know the future but I know Who holds the future." That reflects the words of Jeremiah. He didn't know what tomorrow would bring, but he knew that in the morning he'd experience a fresh supply of God's faithfulness. Burn this truth onto your life's hard drive so that when difficult times come, you can access and use it.

THE SHORT VIEW VERSUS THE LONG VIEW — LOOK AHEAD

ROMANS 8:18-28

"How could something so terrible be good?" This was the question a grieving husband asked as he stood a few steps from the single white casket containing the bodies of his wife and seven-month-old adopted daughter. The people in that crowded church, the reporters who were witnessing an event so unlike their typical assignments, the unseen number who either via the Internet or on some broadcast channels were drawn by the soft, steady voice of Jim Bowers to ask the same question. They were drawn to ponder that question, one that rose from the confusion and rush of events that brought them to that funeral one April night. How could anyone talk about good in the midst of such a tragedy?

One news report described that tragic day this way:

For Jim and Roni Bowers, the plane ride high above the Amazon River was a welcome respite from their rewarding but rigorous life as missionaries. They'd gone to the border town of Leticia, Colombia, with their six-year-old son, Cory, to get a Peruvian visa for their newly adopted daughter, seven-month-old Charity. And now they were enjoying a breathtaking view of the rain-forest canopy during a three-hour return trip to their mission base in Iquitos, Peru. For days, Jim had been happily anticipating the opportunity to gaze down upon the fifty-six villages where he'd been spreading the Gospel by houseboat. "I get a better feel for how they're situated and their full size and location on the river," he e-mailed a friend, Pastor Terry Fulk, back in Fruitport, Michigan. Jim was just where he wanted to be—in the copilot's seat at 4,000 feet, feeding his infant daughter Cheerios. But as he looked out the window to his right, Bowers got a start. There, flying below him on the right side of the Cessna 185, was a Peruvian fighter jet.[1]

In a matter of moments, two lives would be lost and the lives of the three others in the plane would be changed forever, the result of what many would consider a tragic mistake.

Jim sensed trouble. It seemed best to hand Charity back to his wife. The pilot, Kevin Donaldson, radioed the control tower in Iquitos for information. He wanted to find out what the fighter was doing. Then the jet opened fire. "They are killing us!" he yelled into the open microphone as bullets ripped into his leg and smoke filled the cabin. He cut off the fuel to the engine and began to dive for the river while Jim grabbed a fire extinguisher to spray the flames. Then he reached back to help his wife and daughter. But there was nothing he could do to help them now. A single bullet had hit his wife in the back, exited her chest, and entered the baby's head. Both had died instantly.

Some people never recover from an experience like that. The physical wounds might heal, but the emotional scars? Never. As the event fades into the past, it stays a present reality, becoming inescapable.

There are questions I never ask prisoners. My trips into the prison were for ministry, not for satisfying curiosity. But one day a question went through my mind. My friend Carlton and I were between fences. We'd passed through one set of gates, and we were walking in an open area, heading toward the guardhouse when the thought of escape came to mind.

A quick glance around. The high fences were topped with barbed wire and the guardhouses were elevated and positioned for maximum visibility—and a clear shot if necessary. The quick question that I'd never ask an inmate flashed through my mind then: "Have you ever thought about escaping?"

In our own prisons, escape looks impossible, both physically and emotionally. Sleep only replays the images. Events only remind us of the pain. The passing of time only deepens the wounds. Soon the fences are high, the wire sharp, and we find ourselves in a place as impossible to break out of as the facility where I was that day.

Living by the Long View

GOD'S WORD HELPS us escape. To this point, we've seen a variety of important truths—from literal prisoners in the Bible, from a prophet facing an invading army that enslaves many, and from a captive in exile. These truths are steps that can help us make sense of life struggles, find God's faithfulness, and help us survive. You sing, have faith, remember, pray, and trust. And now you live by the long view.

Sometimes as I'm studying, I'll jot down this sequence of strokes: SV/LV. That's all it takes. Those four letters and a slash in the center are reminders of the important truth that keeps a person from being captured by his immediate situation. They remind me of these words: short view versus long view. This truth is repeated in Scripture and it needs to be lived out in life. We must not live by the short view. God wants us to live by the long view.

Your current situation will change. For the follower of Christ, that change ultimately will be for the better. Perhaps the cancer won't be healed now, but it will be totally healed when we enter God's presence. The disability that has hindered will be removed in the presence of Jesus. Those trying times that seem so long will ultimately be seen as fleeting, even miniscule in duration compared to the eternal joy of heaven. The liberating effects of this truth can be known only by those who take their eyes from the immediate to focus on the eternal.

A few months after those tragic events in Peru, sitting in a motel room near where he and his son were living, Jim and I had a time to talk. I asked, "Did you go through a time of saying to God, 'Why did this happen'?"

"Actually, not," he said, "and I'm not at all going to take the credit for that. God just spared me from having those questions. Many people have asked why and have asked me if I'm asking why, as you have. And I haven't come to that point, and I figure now, I won't. In my case, it's been really different than most people who lose a loved one—possibly in obscurity or who don't see much result from it. And in my case, there have been just uncountable stories. I just couldn't relay all the things I've heard about the good that has happened. So seeing that and recognizing that it's from God, it doesn't allow me any room to ask that question why God would allow it, because I can see clearly why He allowed it in my case."

Through our conversation that day—from when we first met at the airport as he drove me to where I'd be staying, and in our time recording an interview—Jim spoke very basic themes, threads of thought woven together, forming a picture of biblical truth lived out in trying times. He spoke of heaven, of prayer, and of God's purposes, but not in the sense of a carefully constructed outline. No, these things just flowed from the heart of a man who loves God, loves His Word, and seeks to live for Him. I listened as he spoke, listened again as I replayed the tape from the interview, talked with mutual acquaintances, and read a multitude of newspaper, magazine, and Internet reports.

Then the loose threads came together, the picture emerged, a very clear and unmistakable one. While most will focus attention on the tragedy, we need to focus on the truth Jim was living out. While others look at a WWJD bracelet, here was a man who was doing what Jesus would do without thinking, just by being what God wants and living what God's Word teaches. The result was that in the midst of hurt, he could see that God is good. His words resonated with the truths of Romans 8. He was living by the long view, not the short view.

The Long View Looks to Heaven

Life hurts. That's the sound-byte version, a bumper sticker–sized reworking of a phrase Kent Hughes wrote in his commentary on Romans when he spoke of "the inescapable reality of the pain of human existence."[2] Or in the short form: life hurts. Paul knew that. When his ship was not sinking or he was not being stoned or robbed, he was being whipped to within an inch of his life. Paul wasn't speaking poetically when he told the Galatians, "Finally, let no one cause me trouble, for I bear on my body the marks of Jesus" (6:17).

We all have this in common. Our hurts vary, but they're still hurts. We're all fellow sufferers. Our suffering grows from the muck of life where we were planted right from the beginning. Strength-sapping, emotion-draining, soul-staining muck. Troubles come and go, some move in and stay, like unwelcome guests with no anticipated departure, no end in sight. We know this. What we don't know is what to do about it.

Paul tells us what to do. The strength we need when life hurts is found when we get our eyes off the muck and onto the glory that lies ahead. Paul spoke of heaven when he said, "I consider that our present sufferings are not worth comparing with the glory that will be revealed in us" (Romans 8:18). Paul had thought it over carefully, weighed the evidence, and came to the conclusion that the pain of now was not worth comparing with the glory that is coming. No matter what we've gone through, are presently going through, or will go through, the sum total is not worth comparing with the glory that awaits us. We can compare a thimble of water with the sea, Hughes says, but we cannot compare our sufferings with the coming glory.

And it's not just us. Creation itself, Paul says, "waits in eager expectation" (verse 19), stands on tiptoes, looking forward to redemption because it too has become a sufferer. And there is hope!

It also "will be liberated from its bondage to decay and brought into the glorious freedom of the children of God" (verse 21). But in the meantime it groans like a woman in labor. We enjoy the pictures of newborns, but any husband risks his life by showing around pictures of his wife in labor. Agony doesn't make a terrific picture.

The church itself groans—the body of Christ has the same struggle as Paul himself—as does creation in its entirety. The apostle keeps building the case that life hurts by pointing to this cosmos-wide distress, focusing attention now on us as God's redeemed people. We groan, creation groans, and so do all those who are waiting for the redemption of our bodies (see 8:23). Though we strain, we look ahead—standing again on our tiptoes, wanting, hoping—not quite able to see, but knowing that glory is coming.

Too often, though, we live shortsighted. We only see the immediate and we don't even consider the eternal. Our eyes are focused on the muck. Our bodies are reminders of the pain. Our spirits sag because life hurts. "Same old, same old," we like to say.

But get your eyes to focus beyond the eighteen inches in front of you, lift them up to see eternity. The hope of heaven is meant to be more than a theological point discussed in a book on doctrine. It calms the troubled heart by drawing our attention to the glory that awaits us.

On the night before the Cross, Jesus knew His disciples were struggling. Following Jesus had become more like a careening roller coaster ride as they'd moved from the days of wildly accepting crowds to intense opposition and threatening circumstances surrounding them in Jerusalem that week. To their storm-tossed hearts, Jesus addressed the familiar words, "Do not let your hearts be troubled" (John 14:1). Then He told them about heaven. Seldom is the hope of heaven too strong; most often it is far too weak.

In 1941, C. S. Lewis preached the sermon, "The Weight of Glory." In it he said,

> *Some day, God willing we shall get in . . . Indeed, if we consider the unblushing promises of reward and the staggering*

nature of the reward promised in the Gospels, it would seem that our Lord finds our desires not too strong, but too weak. We are half-hearted creatures fooling about with drink and sex and ambition when infinite joy is offered us, like an ignorant child who wants to go on making mud pies in a slum because he cannot imagine what is meant by the offer of a holiday at the sea.[3]

We see the muck when we need to be looking to glory, lifting our eyes from the dirt toward the heavens. The frustrations and difficulties of life can sometimes all but erase the image of that glory for us. If we shift our focus away from the hard times, the glory can all but erase the image of the frustrations and difficulties. The image may never be totally erased this side of heaven, but the thought of eternal glory can ease the pain and sustain us.

The hope of heaven sustained Jim. The plane crashed into the Amazon, and people familiar with the dynamics of landing a burning pontoon plane without use of the rudder (due to the pilot's wounded legs) are still amazed that anyone survived, let alone escaped the burning wreckage. Donaldson was bleeding profusely, yet he was able to put Jim's six-year-old son, Cory, on his back and exit the plane. Jim recovered the bodies of his wife and daughter.

As the reality of their situation became clear to Jim, he didn't quote Romans 8:18. But he lived it when he told his son that his mom and new sister were in heaven. "Now they won't hurt anymore," he said.

Later Jim would say to me, "The biggest encouragement is the fact that Roni and Charity are fine. Not only are they fine, they're much better off than we are. And I don't feel bad for them. And I shouldn't want them back because they're standing right now in the presence of the Lord."

The Long View Prays

"In the same way," Paul writes, "the Spirit helps us in our weakness. We do not know what we ought to pray for, but the Spirit himself intercedes for us with groans that words cannot express" (8:26).

Notice the first phrase, "in the same way." Paul isn't changing subjects—he's still dealing with the issue of how to handle the difficulties of life. He tells us to focus on the glory that is to come, then to pray. These are two of the helps He gives us for the hard times, two helps that not only do assist us but also remind us of the goodness of God. In the middle of the worst, He holds out the hope of heaven and the Spirit helps us pray.

Catch the convicting reality of this statement by Kent Hughes: "If we are honest with ourselves we must all admit there are times when we cannot pray. There have been times when my children were so desperately ill and the urgency so great that I could scarcely converse with God."[4] It may be that in the shock of a situation our brains are paralyzed, not literally but most definitely unable to move, to think. Our eyes fix on nothing and our thoughts freeze. We can't form words and we can't or won't until—until who knows when.

Yet we know we should pray! Though devastated, hurt, distressed, weakened, ignorant, and silent; or perhaps we find ourselves so discouraged that we don't have the will to pray. "What's the use?" we say by our silence. And we stay silent, even before God.

Our minds shudder at the thought of hearing the sound of bullets tearing through the fabric of a small plane, the sputtering choking off of the engine, and then that feeling of falling. You've felt a roller coaster topping the first hill, plunging downward, and then the inward effects of such a fast drop. Or maybe you've been on a commercial jetliner when it hit turbulence: you feel that dip, a moment of falling, but then you know the plane is flying again.

This time, though, it was only the feeling of falling as the plane plummeted to earth, the pilot struggling to land on the river below. The Peruvian fighter jet made a few fast, low passes over their plane. The flames died out and the three survivors climbed onto the capsized, half-submerged wreck. Belts and socks became tourniquets and the middle of the river became a place of prayer. As they waited for help to come, Jim, Kevin, and Cory prayed out loud for God to take care of them. Not the expected, typical, or desired call to prayer. We prefer praying in a pew, with gentle organ accompaniment.

God not only gives us the privilege of prayer, but for the hard times He's given us His Spirit Who helps us pray. He *helps*. The word means "to take hold with another," and implies working together and sharing in the same work. Martha used this word when she asked for Mary's help in the kitchen when she said, in essence, "Tell her to help me by taking hold of her end of the task." This kind of help is like two people carrying a log, one at each end. The Holy Spirit lays hold of our burden, helping us carry it, helping us pray.

We may be ignorant, not knowing what to pray, Paul says, but the Spirit knows. In other words, God teaches us that the Holy Spirit expresses those things we feel but cannot articulate. He says the things we want to say but can't. In those moments when we're weak and ignorant, He's strong and knows even the will of God. Paul says that "the Spirit intercedes for the saints in accordance with God's will" (8:27). God's goodness is evident. Not only does He give us the hope of glory, but the help we need to pray in the difficult times of life.

I walked out of my office, e-mail in hand, to enlist others to pray that afternoon when news was first sent to me of the tragedy in Peru. The call to prayer began to go out around the world, hastened by the speed of electronic communication. Others heard and announced it in the churches they attended, spoke of it in small groups, and passed it on. The news media picked up the story and for an extraordinary space of ten days kept it at the top of the news cycle. God's people were constantly reminded and many continually prayed.

The Long View Remembers God's Purposes

Now we come to the part of Romans 8 that's most familiar: "And we know that in all things God works for the good of those who love him, who have been called according to his purpose" (verse 28). And perhaps we're a bit surprised. So often this essentially is all we hear sliced out and quoted. Hard times come and people say, "Remember Romans 8:28!"

Ever notice the first word in this verse? It's the word "and." That's a conjunction, a connecting word, an indication that this is not the beginning of a thought but a continuation of one. Something comes before it. So we need to back up a bit and read about prayer, a section that begins with the words, "In the same way." Because that phrase is making a comparison, it also functions as a conjunction of sorts, joining these verses with those preceding. So we back up a bit more and read about heaven.

Do you see what so many of us miss here? This chapter contains help for the hard times that is more than one verse long. The help God provides is multifaceted, future-oriented, Spirit-assisted, purpose-centered help. When we read only one verse, we rob ourselves of the fullness of what God has given to us. It is like eating pumpkin pie and then learning that there was whipped cream in the refrigerator. The pie was good, but think about what you missed. To help us through the hard times God gives us the hope of heaven, the help of the Spirit in our praying, and an understanding of His purpose in our lives.

The Boundaries

ROMANS 8:28 IS a verse of boundaries and at the same time one without boundaries. Understanding both allows God's Word to accomplish its intended purpose. It's a verse with a specific focus, one that Paul wants us to know as he writes of God's purpose: the providential care of the life of a believer.

The first boundary is that this is not a truth for all people at all times. The boundary the verse sets is this: It is for the people of God, "those who love him, who have been called according to His purpose." These are not the people who have a fondness toward God or an attachment to religious things, but those who love Him. Love is much more than emotion or fondness. Love responds, yes with joy and happiness, but also with obedience, service, a desire to do what the loved one asks. Suppose a person lives his life without any acknowledgment of God. He lives life on his own terms, and whatever religious observance he practices is constructed of his own ideas, built on his own will. A disaster hits and a well-meaning person quotes this verse. But that's outside the boundaries.

Some people might call this harshness, but it's not. This is simply a God-determined boundary that encourages those who are followers of Him and that can draw others to Him as the God who loves, cares, and works even in the midst of our difficulties. This verse is often quoted because it brings so much comfort. But it's a comfort available to those who are God's children. To those who have responded positively to the call of God, this verse is like a warm truth on a cold, wintry day.

The second boundary is that *good* is what God defines as good. Our idea of good doesn't always match up with God's. A trial comes into our lives that may seem bad, but God sees the good that will be the outcome. It will be good. The first chapter of the book of James helps us understand this. We might have judged an experience as bad, but God says ultimately good will result—good as He defines it. This isn't a cop-out on God's part, where He avoids giving us what's really good or reinterprets things to do some kind of theological double-speak, whereby bad is called good. It *is* good. Understanding this involves an aspect of trust as well as surrender. We must trust that God really does know what is good and we must surrender to His accomplishing of good in our lives.

This verse doesn't say that all things are good, but that all things are used by God for our ultimate good. That's an important distinction. Sometimes when difficulties come, people will pronounce the troubles *themselves* as good, citing this verse as proof. Read what it says. It does say "all things," but it doesn't say that "all things are good." It says that "in all things God works for the good. . . . " Those things may indeed be horrible, but God can work through them.

The third boundary is fact, not emotion. "And we know." The verse does not say, "and we feel all things to be good." Our situations

101

may not feel good at all. They may feel exactly the opposite, like we're being ground down or destroyed. The verse doesn't even say that "we see the good," because it just may be beyond our ability to see how something good could come out of our lives right at the moment.

James Montgomery Boice pointed out:

> *Paul was no sentimentalist. He had been persecuted, beaten, stoned, and shipwrecked. He had been attacked and consistently slandered by the Gentiles as well as by his own countrymen. Paul did not go around saying how wonderful the world was or how pleasant his missionary endeavors had been. On the contrary, he reported that he had been "hard pressed on every side... perplexed... and struck down." But Paul came through the things that pressed down and perplexed him precisely because he knew that God was working out his own greater and good purposes through these events.*[5]

Bottom line, Paul knew. Getting pounded with the surf after a shipwreck probably didn't feel like "good," but Paul knew it was not a matter of what he felt. He knew God would use that shipwreck ultimately for good, which brings us to the part of the verse without boundaries.

Without Boundaries

"ALL THINGS." EVERYTHING that has ever happened to us, or that can possibly happen to us, or that will happen to us—the end result is inevitably and utterly for our good. Even the worst things will be, by the work of God, made to be good. Perhaps the good will be in the results, perhaps in the lessons we learn, perhaps in the testimonies that result, perhaps in ways we just can't imagine. But it will be good because God works in all things.

Jim saw that. In working through all the challenges of his devastating loss, he said,

"Another thing that has helped me is to realize that my faith in this case hasn't been shaken. It has been stretched and definitely strengthened. And I thank the Lord for that—for allowing me to be closer to Him than ever before and to see my friends and others much closer to the Lord than before. I'm amazed to hear all the stories through e-mails and phone calls of how God has brought people back to Himself and has awakened people and given them opportunities to witness. I've received quite a number of testimonies about how people have been saved. There are a few who have chosen to become missionaries because of this. So many things that point directly to God working in people's hearts . . . "[6]

Paul spoke of heaven, of prayer, and of God's purposes—and he said it all with the long view in mind. So did Jim. And that's the way it should be. The Word speaks, we hear, we take it in. And it becomes our words, part of our lives. You need to listen to what the Bible teaches, and learn it. But there is yet another step. You must live it.

Perhaps now, you'll never look at Romans 8 the same. Perhaps the next time someone quotes Romans 8:28, that first word, *And*, will remind you that there's great help for the hard times. The hope of heaven, the help of the Spirit as we pray, the hand of God taking the all things of our lives and bringing about good ultimately. Learn to look ahead.

Is God good? He is; He certainly is. Now and forever.

Study Guide

Part 1 — Getting into the Word

Prayer: Jim's story captured the headlines for several weeks in the spring of 2001. Throughout that time, the media coverage consistently revealed a man whose focus wasn't on the immediacy of his situation, but one that looked ahead. Jim Bowers lives by the long view. Do you? Ask God to help this lesson change the way you view events.

Reading and Hearing God's Word: Romans 8 needs to be read in its entirety. Some people like to memorize that whole chapter for all the rich truth it contains. Perhaps you'd like to do that as well. As you go through it, watch for verses or ideas that strike a responsive chord today. Allow the primary section of Romans 8 to expand your understanding beyond verse 28.

Understanding God's Word: Read Romans 8:18-28 again. Underline any key phrases or ideas that seem especially meaningful to you. Then look back through these verses and answer the following questions:

1. In verse 18, Paul mentions "present sufferings." What might these have been?
2. Which two things are specifically said to be "groaning"? What is their shared hope?
3. List the benefits of the Spirit interceding for us. (They're found in verses 26-27.)
4. What "boundaries" of verse 28 are mentioned in the rest of the chapter?

Meditating on God's Word: Write a brief summary of a meaningful verse or idea you noticed. Why did you choose this particular verse? Is there a specific way it applies to your life today?

Part 2 — Taking the Word into My World

Romans 8:28 is one of the most often-quoted verses, especially in times of difficulty. It's a great truth, but you now know that it's just part of a great passage offering encouragement.

1. Consider the emphasis Paul puts on heaven in this passage. It's easier to live dominated by the present, forgetting the future. But the long view pulls your heart to eternity. How certain are you that heaven will be your final destination? If you're even slightly unsure, what steps do you need to take to be certain? Do you know someone who can answer your questions about heaven?
2. The long view prays. Describe your prayer habits. What do you need to do to improve?

3. Are God's purposes and our purposes always the same? Have you surrendered to His leadership of your life?

Part 3 — Grabbing Hold

Write out a prayer, using each of the major points of this lesson to create a paragraph in your prayer. Perhaps right now you're struggling with events affecting your life. Center your prayer on the issues that are drawing your focus to the short view. Make your prayer one that pulls your heart to the long view.

Now a test. You haven't done this for a few chapters! Review the vital truths you've learned so far:

Chapter 1 : _____

Chapter 2 : _____

Chapter 3 : _____

Chapter 4 : _____

Chapter 5 : _____

Chapter 6 : _____

IN THE MEANWHILE — WAIT

GENESIS 37:36

Her testimony began in a simple, straightforward way. "This past August, I lost my fiancé, Jonathan Leach, to a car accident. Jon and I dated for almost six years. He was my best friend, my boyfriend, and eventually my fiancé. We came to Cedarville four years ago with many plans and dreams, and they were all swept away within a few minutes.[1]

With those few sentences, Andrea Dufour began her challenge to the student body during senior chapel just prior to her graduation from Cedarville University—an event that took place as scheduled, but not as planned, because Jon wasn't there.

We make plans and anticipate the future. Andrea and Jonathan began dating and determined that theirs was a romance that would last. They'd go to college, graduate together, then on to a wedding, a marriage, and the establishing of a home. The graduation took place but not as expected. In August before their senior year, Andrea, Jonathan, and a friend were traveling together from Delaware to Tennessee. They'd traveled only seven miles from Jon's home when the accident occurred. She'd survived along with their friend, but Jon didn't.

"I woke up in the hospital, asking for Jonathan. I knew something was wrong because he wasn't there with me. I can still picture my dad weeping over me in the hospital room, telling me that Jonathan had died. I was numb and didn't know how to feel. I was filled with memories of him.

"I wasn't able to attend my fiancé's funeral because I was still in the ICU, and doctors weren't sure if my condition was stable enough. When I found out that I missed Jon's funeral, it broke my heart."

At first it was so hard, she said. "When I returned home, my heart felt like it had broken into a million pieces. I wanted to pick up the phone to call Jon and ask how his day went or to tell him something that had happened to me that day. At that point, I had the choice to either become bitter or to trust God. I knew that Jon would never have wanted me to become bitter. A picture of our last night together flashed in my mind. It was a Wednesday night prayer meeting and we were praying together. I can still hear Jon asking God for His will in both of our lives."

An inmate knows the meaning of being shackled. A guard attaches handcuffs to a chain around the waist that reaches down and encircles the ankles. And the prisoner can't do much more than shuffle. He can't move forward without constantly being reminded that the chains are holding him back. He might want to run, but he can hardly walk.

Life events can be like handcuffs, holding you back, holding you in their grip, keeping you from moving forward. Andrea faced that possibility.

So what is the rest of the story? We want happy endings but her words that day carried only the reality of an ongoing time of adjustment, of an unsure future. Andrea returned to the campus where so many scenes brought back memories of her and Jonathan's years together there as students, and by God's grace she completed her studies and received her degree.

When the present was the future it didn't look like this for her. It didn't involve standing alone before her classmates, her mind now filled more with images of the past than of the present. Yet Andrea also realized that meanwhile, the peace she felt in her heart was from God, a gift to carry her through the days ahead. She drew strength from the love of family and friends, but especially from the truths of the Word of God.

Living in the "Meanwhile" of Life

ANDREA WASN'T THE first young person to find herself living in the "meanwhile" of life. Sometimes that's where we live, in the "meanwhile." William Ireland noted that word in the story of Joseph. At the time his brothers were explaining what they said had happened to Joseph, the Scripture quickly cuts from that scene to what was happening in Egypt: "Meanwhile, the Midianites sold Joseph in Egypt to Potiphar" (Genesis 37:36). Remember the old grade-B westerns? They seemed to always have the line, "Meanwhile, back at the ranch." Someone said that this verse reminded him of that. The attention is focused one place but something is going on in another! Now the attention is shifted to what is going on in Egypt. It doesn't sound like much is happening—Joseph is sold to Potiphar—but the door is slightly open. There is more to come. As Yogi Berra is quoted as saying, "It ain't over till it's over." There is more to come.

When a crisis hits, our praying may escalate—or at least it should. In that time, we might cling tenaciously to the truth that God is good and that His goodness is at work all the time. We've held up examples such as Paul and Silas and examples from today like Tim and Leanne. We've allowed the prophet Habakkuk to teach us the truth that "the righteous man will live by his faith." We don't live by our sight; we don't make decisions and judgments on the basis of what we see; we live by faith in God.

Then we move through an array of passages that can be summarized in a sentence: "Remember to trust the faithful God who helps us in our hard times." In fact, learn that sentence, and ponder the Scriptures it's constructed from: Remember (see Psalm 137) to trust (see Psalm 13) the faithful God (see Lamentations 3) who helps us in our hard times (see Romans 8). When that truth really sinks in—reinforced by the teaching of Scripture and the testimony of faithful witnesses—then we'll be able to say, as we live by the long view, that God is good.

When things are going well, our praise may escalate—or at least it should. Perhaps God heals the cancer and we can give testimony to our answered prayers. Or a contract is renewed, the business turns around, and we give thanks to Him. You start to think about the biggest thing in your life right now and a smile comes over your face because it's all going just fine. All those truths about God's goodness, all those testimonies don't have to sink in very far because right now, life shows that God is good.

Sold!

But it's not always that way. Life doesn't always seem great, but it doesn't always seem like the bottom of the pits either. Sometimes we find ourselves in between—in the meanwhile, back-at-the-ranch kind of time. How do we know and show that God is good in those times?

So, meanwhile, the Midianites sold Joseph. So what? Let his story sink in; he was a person whose "meanwhile" began when he was a teenager and continued for years. Let it sink in and see how he lived, how he didn't give up on God.

Jacob probably felt like life had finally settled down for him. His parents have died, he's reconciled with his brother Esau, and he's moved back "home." He's even straightened out his relationship with God, although he does walk with a limp now. So Moses writes, "This is the account of Jacob" (37:2), and the next word is "Joseph." The rest of Genesis is more Joseph than Jacob. The focus moves from Jacob to his seventeen-year-old son, the next to the youngest of his boys, who's out working the flocks with his stepbrothers. Joseph is the favored son—and as soon as a dad starts to show favoritism, conflict and tension with the siblings soon follows.

Joseph stirred the fires of resentment that were already heating up when he brought Dad a bad report about his stepbrothers. The Bible doesn't say what he said or why he gave it. We just know that it didn't help bring harmony to the family dinner table. Then Joseph added fuel to the fire. He had a dream indicating that in the future he wouldn't just be the favorite son, but the one his brothers would bow down to.

The fire has been stirred, fuel added, and flames fanned by this. Joseph's brothers said to him, "'Do you intend to reign over us? Will you actually rule us?' And they hated him all the more because of his dream and what he had said" (37:8). His next dream even upset his father, who rebuked him. "'What is this dream you had? Will your mother and I and your brothers actually come and bow down to the ground before you?'" (verse 10). Now his brothers are just plain jealous of Joseph.

For Joseph, the present and the future looked good. He had position and promise. It looked like everything was working for him. Then suddenly, it looked like everything was against him. About the only way to explain what happens next is to note that Jacob was out of touch with his own family. He was so unaware of the simmering rage of the brothers that he put Joseph into a situation of great danger. He sent Joseph to check on them. They were grazing their father's flocks at a place about fifty miles away, near Shechem, the city where his daughter was raped and the men of the city killed by two of his sons. Perhaps that's why Jacob was concerned.

The brothers could see Joseph coming. And Dad wasn't along to protect his favorite son. The only people who would really know what happened would be this band of brothers. As he approached, they plotted to kill him, and to cover up his death with a story of a wild beast, a devoured carcass, a bloody coat. So they grabbed him and threw him into a cistern.

If you think you're in the pits, consider this one. A cistern in Joseph's day would have been a hole in the ground, dug into the dry rock of the land, perhaps lined by limestone. Rainwater would be channeled into it. But they threw Joseph into a dry cistern. The Hebrew word *shalak* here is very specific. If you took the body of a dead person and threw it into a grave, this is the word you would use. Or if you took a person who was not yet dead, but you intended for him to die in that hole, this is the word. They didn't take Joseph, their "dear little brother," and lower him into a hole for safekeeping. They threw him into a pit they intended to be his grave, rolled the stone over the opening, and then sat down and ate their lunch. They'd become cold-hearted killers.

If you remember this story, one of the brothers figures out a way to keep his brother from dying but also to make a little profit off of him. So he convinces the others to sell Joseph as a slave to a group of Midian slave traders passing by. Joseph shields his eyes as the stone is rolled back and light floods into the cistern. He struggles to his feet and looks up toward the faces staring at him, bargaining over him, leaving him wondering what is next. Seventeen years old, traveling with slaves. He didn't understand their language, and they were taking him to a place he didn't know. Quickly, Joseph moved from a position of being most favored to living with the expectation of a day when he'd be placed on the block and auctioned off like a piece of merchandise. He was certainly in the "meanwhile" of his life.

The story moves back home, telling us about Judah and Tamar. Judah had suggested selling Joseph; now his life goes on with no thought about Joseph. He picks up a prostitute who turns out to be his daughter-in-law. Meanwhile, back in Egypt, when it seemed that nothing was going on, God was there, working in the meanwhile of Joseph's life. The Lord was with him, the Lord gave him success, and the blessing of the Lord was on him. God hasn't deserted Joseph and Joseph hasn't deserted God.

Set Apart

Joseph shows us the human side of living out the truth that God is good, all the time. Living this way isn't a one-sided, all-of-God, none-of-us safety net arrangement where God is relegated to being our cosmic bail-bondsman, always getting us out of our jams. Instead, it's the fleshing out of the basic truth of salvation as Paul states it in Ephesians 2:8: "For it is by grace you have been saved, through faith." Yes, we're saved by grace through faith. Sometimes we treat Scripture like a pie, taking only the slice we like or want and settle for it just like we do Romans 8:28. But again, that means we miss out on the other help God gives us. When we read only verse 8 of Ephesians 2, we miss the truth that we're "created in Christ Jesus to do good works" (verse 10). God's sovereign plan is that salvation makes a difference in how we live.

So we don't just sit back and expect God to be good all the time, taking care of us all the time, curing all that ails us all the time. No. Like Joseph, we live out the truth. Knowing God makes a difference in our lives.

This showed in the way Joseph lived. It looked as though God had forgotten him. He knew his brothers had abandoned him and had sold him off to his death. Yet at this time when it looked like there was no hope, Joseph lived his life in a way that set him apart. The way he conducted himself as a slave and fulfilled his responsibilities led to promotion by Potiphar. God's hand was in this promotion. "The LORD was with Joseph and he prospered, and he lived in the house of his Egyptian master. When his master saw that the LORD was with him and that the LORD gave him success in everything he did, Joseph found favor in his eyes and became his attendant" (Genesis 39:2-4). Potiphar wanted Joseph to be close by, taking care of him.

Set Back

Then Potiphar put Joseph in charge of everything he owned. As Potiphar looks at Joseph, he doesn't see a rebellious slave seething with anger at his brothers and plotting escape to get revenge. Not at all. Instead Potiphar looks at him and says, "This is the kind of guy I want to promote." God gives us the whole story here. Joseph's good fortunes aren't simply a matter of his good looks or of his ability. It's a matter of God at work in Joseph's life and Joseph remaining faithful to God. He experienced the goodness of God in the midst of slavery. Later in this same chapter, it happens again. God was with Joseph in prison, and He blesses him in a way that the warden puts Joseph in charge.

Have you ever noticed how often God uses prison scenes to teach us? If you were asked to name a few, you'd probably come up with some obvious ones, such as Joseph from this chapter. Now look back over this book. Paul and Silas were in prison. Habakkuk was in the nation at a time when it faced captivity. The unknown psalmist who could not sing was in forced exile, experiencing the captivity Habakkuk saw coming. Jeremiah knew confinement. And even David was a potential prisoner—if Saul had captured him he probably would have become a death row inmate. Lessons learned in the darkest times can yield the brightest light.

At a time when Joseph could have been rebellious, uncooperative, manipulating everything for his gain, sloughing off, and doing as little as possible to get by, he excelled. He could have fostered a bad attitude and become a pain to all those around him, but he didn't. Those are not the things God wants even when we're living in our "meanwhiles."

And Joseph maintained his purity before God and man. Potiphar had noticed Joseph and so had his wife. Her words were direct: "Come to bed with me!" (39:7). She didn't say it once but over and over and over. One day when everyone was out of the house—maybe even by her design—she grabbed hold of Joseph and said, again, "Come to bed with me!" (verse 12).

"No," he replied. He already had told her, "How then could I do such a wicked thing" (verse 9). This time he ran, leaving behind his cloak in her hand.

Potiphar was probably the chief executioner of Egypt. That's a guy you don't want to mess around with, nor with his wife. If he says, "Off with your head," your head is off. It's amazing that Potiphar didn't execute Joseph. He must have believed in Joseph's innocence. The best evidence was the life Joseph had lived before him for a long time before this false accusation. Joseph did what was right and trusted God for the outcome.

Like Joseph, whatever our situation, we must live committed to God. No matter what's said about us, people will look at how we live and see the difference. We must not serve God only in the good times, but in all times. I appreciate these words written by a single woman, a medical doctor serving the Lord in some very difficult situations. She wrote:

> *When stretched, I was strengthened;*
> *When weak, I was empowered.*
> *When irritated, I was convicted.*
> *When sick, I was refreshed.*
> *When pressured, I was helped:*
> *When uncertain, I was encouraged.*
> *Whenever . . . God is always there.*
> —Dr. Miriam Wheeler[2]

Forgetful and Fruitful

HOW WE LIVE while we wait demonstrates that we really believe God is good all the time. So does what we say. Joseph doesn't say much in most of the chapters that record his life. But what he does say is memorable and insightful. To Potiphar's wife, his words reflect a commitment to purity and an accountability to God. "How then could I do such a wicked thing and sin against God?" (39:9). Before the Pharaoh, who considered himself to be god, Joseph spoke of the true God. Pharaoh wanted Joseph to do for him what he had done for the cupbearer and baker, to interpret a dream. Joseph said, "I cannot . . . but God will give Pharaoh the answer he desires" (41:16). He speaks so confidently and clearly of how God reveals, decides, and carries out His plan that Pharaoh starts saying the same things! "Since God has made all this known to you" (verse 39) are the words that come out of Pharoah's own mouth.

His Children
Perhaps Joseph's strongest testimony to this point in the narrative is in the naming of his sons. He "named his firstborn Manasseh and

said, 'It is because God has made me forget all my trouble and all my father's household.' The second son he named Ephraim and said, 'It is because God has made me fruitful in the land of my suffering'" (verses 51-52). He had not just endured the "meanwhile" of being in Egypt, nor had he used it as a time to store up grain and anger. Instead, he allowed God to work in his heart so that as a man he could say that God had used the time to help him forget his dysfunctional past and be fruitful in the present.

Wouldn't it have been easier, perhaps more natural, to use the time to be angry and resentful toward God? Or maybe he could choose to ignore God and go on his own way. After all, it did appear that God had let him down, given him false hopes, not lived up to what seemed to be promised. That's one of our great dangers—we get bitter because God doesn't come through in a way we approve of. "Hey, God. If you're so good, why is my life so bad?"

Inscribed on a cellar wall in Germany, where Jews hid from Nazis, were these words: "I believe in the sun even when it is not shining. I believe in love even when feeling it not. I believe in God even when He is silent."[3] Joseph could have written those words. Could you? Joseph's words to his brothers were all of God. "God sent me ahead of you. . . . it was not you who sent me here, but God" (45:5,8); "You intended to harm me, but God intended it for good to accomplish what is now being done, the saving of many lives" (50:20). Joseph knew that God is good all the time—even in the "meanwhiles" of life.

His Family

One other thing from the life of Joseph challenges us to trust the faithfulness of God all the time. It's his bones. "Joseph said to his brothers, 'I am about to die. But God will surely come to your aid and take you up out of this land to the land he promised'. . . . And Joseph made the sons of Israel swear an oath and said, 'God will surely come to your aid, and then you must carry my bones up from this place" (verses 24-25). Talk about faith! He so believed the promise of God that he made his family swear to take his bones with them when God delivered them.

Four centuries would pass before Moses would stand before Pharaoh. What a sight it must have been. A slave nation, not escaping, but sent away, heading east to the land their God had promised them. They trekked for forty years through the rugged desert regions of the Sinai peninsula before one day reaching the east side of the Jordan River. It wasn't necessary to carry food because God provided for their needs every day and gave them a double portion for the Sabbath. But it was necessary for them to carry a casket, probably an Egyptian sarcophagus, elaborate, colorfully decorated, gilded with gold.

Perhaps somewhere along the way the people were watched by one of the bedouins of the desert. The slave nation going by, they probably looked like slaves; they were dressed and equipped like slaves, with no appearance of prosperity. But then comes this phenomenal mummy case. "What did you do, rob a grave before you left Egypt?" the bedouin might ask. "No, that's Joseph," they'd reply. "He's one of us. He knew this day was coming and made us promise to bring him with us." What a story that would make! Actually, what a story that is.

Joseph is a remarkable man to study. When you look at his life you see long stretches where it looked like nothing was going right, when it looked like God was absent. Yet in these times, Joseph stayed steady and true, allowing God to work in the times of pain and in the times of promotion. When his sons were born, when his brothers showed up, and even as he prepared for his death, Joseph could look back and see how God had been good to him all the time.

He could have been imprisoned by his past. The restraints put on him by slave traders, the confinements of being Potiphar's property, and the prison cell he occupied were all real—and in the past. While the past sometimes doesn't let go and becomes its own form of confinement, Joseph the prisoner did not stay imprisoned.

When it comes to living out the Christian life, to being a follower of Jesus, a true disciple, it's something we must do 24/7/365—

every hour of every day of every week of every year. No days off. It's not something we take time off from, and it's got to be something that's more than what we say; it must be what we are and do.

Get hold of this from Joseph. At a time when it looked like God had forgotten him, when his brothers had abandoned him and sent him off to his death, when there appeared to be no hope, God was still at work. And Joseph continued to trust in the faithful God who helps us in the hard times.

He had to wait.

And you might have to wait—which doesn't come easily today. Most of us are impatient, stuck on the instant, the quick. That's why you use your microwave more than a Crockpot. That's why you are adept at ordering dinner in a drive-through lane. It's why you haven't been inside your bank in years, choosing the convenience and speed of the ATM. Life is better lived in the "EZ Pass" lane—no need to even stop to pay a toll on the turnpike!

But not all of life's situations can be resolved in thirty minutes or less. You may need to wait, patiently, and let God work.

Hear a bit more of what Andrea said to her classmates: "By God's grace, I was able to return to Cedarville this past Winter Quarter. It wasn't easy for me, and there's no way I could have done this without God's help. Memories of Jon were everywhere I went. I had memories of him competing with the intramural teams and playing his trumpet in pep band.

"Jeremiah 29:11-13 has given me peace as I graduate and am unsure about my future. 'For I know the plans I have for you,' declares the LORD, 'plans to prosper you and not to harm you, plans to give you hope and a future. Then you will call upon me and come and pray to me, and I will listen to you. You will seek me and find me when you seek me with all your heart.'

"If you remember anything that I have said here, remember that you don't have to form a perfect plan for your life, because God already has one for you."[4]

God is good.

Study Guide

Part 1 — Getting into the Word

Prayer: Have you ever just stayed silent before God? Take time right now to pray simply, "God, help me learn to wait." Perhaps in the quiet of these moments, He'll help you understand some areas in your life where you need to wait, to allow Him to work.

Reading and Hearing God's Word: Read all of Joseph's story in Genesis 37-50. Think of it as a short novel. Catch the plot, the cast of characters, the unexpected twists and turns, as well as the good ending. As you do, notice the long periods of time when Joseph could do nothing but wait.

Understanding God's Word: After you've read these chapters in Genesis, answer the following questions:

1. How long did Joseph "wait"? In Genesis 37:2, he is seventeen years old. Use your Bible to figure out how long it was before he met up with his brothers again. You won't find an exact number but you can get a general idea. Perhaps after you work on it, you can check a Bible reference book to see what it suggests.

2. What are the six dreams found in this story? Notice the amount of time that follows each dream and its complete fulfillment.

3. In Genesis 50:25, what instruction did Joseph give that shows he was still waiting for God to work in the life of the nation?

Meditating on God's Word: Read Genesis 50:20. Think about how Joseph learned this lesson. It wasn't an instant lesson, but one learned over a long period of time.

Part 2 — Taking the Word into My World

Impatience rules! Fast food, microwaves, broadband Internet connection — we are not typically patient people. And sometimes we just don't "get over things." The old phrase, "Time heals all wounds" must have been for a different century. Some of our wounds seem to never heal. Joseph had massive wounds inflicted by his own family but in time they were healed. These next two questions can help bring healing to your old wounds.

1. Write the names of Joseph's sons, along with the meaning of each name.

2. Make a list under Manasseh's name of things Joseph "forgot," and under Ephraim's name, evidence that God had made him fruitful. Add to each list things you need to forget and evidences of God's faithfulness.

Part 3 — Grabbing Hold

Think about the times of your life. How old are you? How many years have you been a Christian? Were there times when God allowed you to wait? Do you face circumstances that still require you to wait? Some things may never be totally resolved in this life but when we live by the long view, we can wait.

GOD NEVER WASTES A HURT — PUT IT IN TO PRACTICE

PSALM 73

Not all stories have happy endings, and we sometimes struggle with that. Our preference is for the fairy tale ending. You know what it is: "And they lived happily ever after." That's a "close but not quite right" kind of phrase. Not every story ends that way. With one change, though, we can make it true: "And they lived happily in the ever after." All of a sudden the perspective leaps from the time-bound physical world we live in to the eternal state, that place beyond earthly life where there's only life for the follower of Christ.

If God always gave happily-ever-after endings in this life, then Steve wouldn't have needed to write and send to friends the pages titled, "In Memory of a Daughter." If all was fair in the sense that we judge fair, he and his wife would never have heard the doctor say they could keep their daughter's body alive, but that there was no longer any real hope. But the doctor did say that, Steve and Ginny did hear it, and they made the decision to let go, for now. She'd been "gone" for a year, home for a day, and now she'd be gone for good.

Stephanie, tall with long blond hair, had just turned twenty. She was one of those straight-A students who enrolled to be a piano performance major at the University of Florida. The school was close enough to home for her parents to see her regularly, until an opportunity came for her to travel for a year of ministry with a Christian music group called "Carpenter's Tools." The welcome at the airport was more than expected, more than most twenty-year-olds even want—especially the "Welcome Home" signs intended to help with the embarrassment. She added to the fun by pretending she didn't know them, but soon the reunion of family and friends was in full swing. "All was well with the world," Steve writes. "Our little girl was back in our care."

Then Stephanie got a headache, one that she said felt like a hammer hitting her head. The pain was intense. She started to cry, then had a mild seizure and lost consciousness—all in about five minutes. The 9-1-1 call was placed, an ambulance run to the hospital, preliminary guesses on the more minor side of things, but a CAT scan was ordered anyway. Still, it seemed like a "take two aspirin and call me in the morning" kind of situation. But it wasn't. It happened so quickly. Home less than a day, there would be no more.

It all seems cruel, senseless, unfair. At times we want to ask— really, it's not asking but accusing—we want to ask God, "Why?" It's more of a "Why!"—an exclamation, not a question. He needs to explain this. The emotions of the moment are negative ones. Sing with Paul and Silas? No way. Habakkuk with his platitudes can keep on walking—we have no desire to hear his pious sounding "live by faith" routine. It doesn't all add up the way it should according to our math, so we refuse to solve the equation. God's goodness doesn't factor in. Instead, faith falters, uncertainty creeps in, and just as we are sometimes unaware of how slippery the walkway has become as the temperature drops on a rainy January night, we soon find ourselves on the black ice of unbelief, no longer on firm footing.

Some teach and some try to believe that life for the Christian is all joy and no pain. That just isn't so. Then that realization gets twisted a bit—the perspective skewered. It seems like we have it tough too much of the time while some of the least godly people have it good. It just doesn't make sense—and the foot starts to slip on the ice of unbelief again. And what we lose is the lesson we've been learning. Yes, life is hard, some times harder than others, but God is good, all the time. And we must put that truth into practice.

I sat in the chaplain's office at the prison waiting for an usher to come for me. Not all times for ministry in the prison were the same. A Saturday morning Bible study allowed me more time to mingle with the inmates. This group met in a classroom, not in the chapel building. The Sunday morning times are the most restricted. I'd sit in the office until ushered in to speak, and once finished, I'd be ushered back to the office. There was very little time allowed for interaction.

Saturday afternoon was somewhere in between. I'd be ushered in—then out, but not back to the office. Instead, I could stand in the hallway at the back of the chapel and greet the men as they left.

Many of the men greeted me with handshakes, but others hugged me. "Blessings on you, brother," "Thanks for the Word," "Pray for me," "God be with you." All words spoken with heartfelt sincerity. My life always seemed so good compared to theirs— except during one particular visit. I was between ministries. More bluntly stated, I was unemployed. Just a few weeks before I'd unex- pectedly been told that there no longer were sufficient funds for my job. And the men of the Church Behind the Walls knew it.

The usher came, took me from the office to the front pew. I'd barely made contact with the seat when another inmate took me by the arm and led me up the three steps onto the platform of the chapel. There sat a single chair.

They made me sit and then said, "Would the rest of the dea- cons and prayer committee please come to the platform now?" Soon I was surrounded by men who had gathered at the front to do one thing: lay hands on me and pray.

The leader told the church, "You know what has happened to our brother. He no longer has a job. We're going to pray that God will provide for him and his family."

And pray they did.

Prison is a hard place. No soft tissues to wipe the eyes. I know, because they handed me a paper towel. I needed it as I returned to my seat in tears. "God is good," they would say. "All the time" their response. And as the one who sometimes led them in saying that, right then I needed to practice it.

The key truth of this book, in a sentence, is: Remember to trust the faithful God who helps us in our hard times. Forget that and the walkway gets a little "iffy." Fail to trust, and the need for taking our steps carefully is real. Consider God unreliable and unfaithful, and the ice forms. He does help us in the hard times. But if we only see the hard times and not His help, our walk takes on treacherous proportions. And this truth must be put into practice.

The Slippery Path

JUST ASK ASAPH. He knew what it was like to nearly lose his footing because life looked better for others than for him. And he lost sight of God's goodness. When he got straightened up again, after his trial of faith, he said, "Surely God is good to Israel, to those who are pure in heart" (Psalm 73:1). He concluded that, "it is good to be near God" (verse 28).

In this psalm, Psalm 73, he writes about the age-old question, "Why do the wicked so often seem to prosper while the godly suffer?" Good question. Nice to hear someone ask it aloud, and especially nice that he asks because he probes deeply into it. In fact, it seems that he probes into the very presence of God to find the answer. From that vantage point, looking at things in the way God sees them, our focus is clearer and we can see things as they really are.

Asaph starts with the conclusion that God is good, and His goodness is especially evident in His actions toward Israel, His people, "to those who are pure in heart." That's key. Many people want a God of cosmic goodness, but no relationship with Him and no obligation toward Him. They just desire a God who pours out good on all and does it all the time. Again though, the boundaries are plain. Romans 8:28 is for those who love God and Psalm 73 is for the people of God. He mentions Israel and those who are pure in heart.

The issue that must be settled before the truths of this psalm, of this book, can be applied is this: your relationship with God. Have you received the gift God offers, salvation through His Son Jesus Christ? And do you live your life in such a way that you can be described as "pure in heart"? This doesn't speak of a sinless life, but of a conscious and consistent striving to live a godly life — to *live* pure in heart.

The Struggle for Footing

In the second verse, Asaph immediately describes his days of a slippery path. "My feet had almost slipped; I had nearly lost my foothold" (verse 2). Think wintertime. A misting rain, just enough to coat the parking lot while you're shopping. The forecasted cold front arrives. But your mind hasn't registered that what looks to be wet is actually ice. As you head back to the car, grocery bags in each arm, your foot slips. You catch yourself with a sudden, upward jerk that wrenches your spine and almost spills the canned goods. Now your steps are more measured.

It can happen physically. It can happen spiritually, too. Asaph struggled for his footing; he was on the verge of a severe fall. And he knows why. It was "the prosperity of the wicked" (verse 3). It didn't make sense to him, and it doesn't make sense to us. This isn't the "Golden Rule" by any means, but it's the general rule that we think exists — God should reward the godly and punish the ungodly. Seems reasonable enough. It's just not reality.

Just as Job 21:7-15 listed the evidence of the good life as seen in the ungodly, Asaph puts together his list as well. The ungodly seem to have no struggles. Instead they have healthy and strong bodies with none of the common burdens most people face. Instead of living in humility and fear before God, the ungodly appear to be proud, violent, callous, and arrogant — even religious, as if heaven is theirs and so is the earth. The crowd goes with them and they live as if God doesn't know what is going on in their lives, or He doesn't care and it just doesn't matter. And they keep getting richer. Live on the basis of what you see and you'll live miserably. Look at what others have and you'll see exactly that—what they have. Like Asaph, you'll notice the fine clothes, nice cars, luxurious lifestyles, haughty attitudes. Then you may also, like the psalmist, begin to wonder, *why try to live a godly life when it seems the better life is an ungodly one?* Feel the ice under your feet? It's forming rather quickly now and if you don't realize it you will slip. Here are Asaph's exact words: "Surely in vain have I kept my heart pure; in vain have I washed my hands in innocence. All day long I have been plagued; I have been punished every morning" (verses 13-14). He's going down. If he keeps thinking that way, his faith will fail and he'll fall.

The Spiritual Illness

This could be called his spiritual illness, one that Asaph later realizes was better kept to himself. He could hurt others with his words. His unresolved doubts might do damage to others, causing them to join him in this dangerous time of evaluation and questioning. Going to someone who will walk alongside us and help us resolve the nagging issues of faith is one thing. But broadcasting them wholesale without concern for the spiritual well-being of others is another—a thing to be avoided. Asaph refrained and later saw that his restraint was good.

The Spiritual Insight

So what keeps him from finding his feet over his head, his back on the ground, his head aching from the pain of impact? "When I tried to understand all this, it was oppressive to me till I entered the sanctuary of God; then I understood their final destiny" (verses 16-17). What transpired was more than going into a building, even if it was the temple, even if it was a place for worship. The spiritual life is lived out in the dimensions of the physical world but the spiritual life doesn't consist of the physical. Going to church doesn't make a difference if all you do is go in the building. Physically entering a sanctuary doesn't give you deeper spiritual insight.

Of course, staying away doesn't help either! What makes the difference is hearing God's truth in that sanctuary, in our times of worship, being guided in deeper insight through God's Word and led by His Holy Spirit. We take our troubled perspectives to God and seek understanding from His Word. Asaph did the same. And what he learned, he shares as the resolution to this troublesome problem.

The solution? Have an eternal perspective.

Far too often, we live time-bound, even though as the children of God we're people of eternity. The here and now looms large before us because it's what we see as we look around. We make judgments too easily on that basis, with an "I see, therefore it is" kind of rationalization. The wicked prosper, the godly don't—and the feet start to slip. But then, the life of the ungodly is more like a dream than reality, Asaph observes, their lives being of little or no consequence.

Asaph was looking at things from God's perspective. He began to again appreciate eternity. This world is not all there is to our existence. We can't live by the short view alone; we must be thinking long view. As Steve stood by that hospital bed, he wanted to ask God to restore his little girl to him and her yearning mother. The doctor had said there was no hope, nothing else could be done. But in Steve's mind, he remembered that he knew "the Healer." So he prayed, asking God to give her life. But he couldn't bring himself to specify where. He had a fear that kept him from asking that—a fear that his own good plan as her earthly father would conflict with the perfect will of her heavenly Father.

Finding Sure Footing

"I DO BELIEVE that Stephanie lives," Steve writes. "I do believe that she is perfectly happy, that she is safe, and that I will see her again."

That's the reality of eternity understood. That's seeing things from God's perspective, not man's. Our feet are on firm ground when the eyes of sight don't have the final word, but instead we decide to live by the eyes of faith.

To live otherwise is like being a dumb animal. "When my heart was grieved and my spirit embittered, I was senseless and ignorant; I was a brute beast before you" (verses 21-22). Asaph wasn't thinking straight. Getting his eyes off the truth of God and onto the situations of other men moved him from firm faith to faltering steps. The good-news part of the psalm comes next as he testifies to the ongoing presence of God—Who holds him, guides him, and will ultimately take him to glory. What wonderful words of testimony then follow: "Whom have I in heaven but you? And earth has nothing I desire besides you" (verse 25). The psalm writer declares that God is the strength of his heart.

Now the matter is settled. Asaph declares with certainty, "it is good to be near God. I have made the Sovereign LORD my refuge; I will tell of all your deeds" (verse 28). Life now will be walked on paths with firm footings. He's flirted with disaster, seen the future, and realized that the best place to be is near God. Asaph makes a conscious decision, based not on the present experiences of others but on future certainties. Perhaps some things are hard, but considered in the light of eternity, the gain far outweighs all pain.

Think of it this way. You have something wrong physically. Pick your pain. How about a defective heart valve. The doctor says you have a choice, sort of. Continue to live with the pain and limitations of a heart unable to function effectively or go through surgery. You don't want me to describe open-heart surgery. Bypass surgery is invasive enough, but it's done on the outside of the heart. Valve replacement means . . . well, let's just leave it there. It sounds too painful.

The pain is for now, and as a surgeon friend says, "A chance to cut is a chance to heal." I sometimes look at my friends with scars on their chests, ask them how they're feeling, and then ask if they think they made the right decision. Every time they answer, "Yes."

The short-term pain was worth going through for the long-term benefits.

Asaph looked around him, saw people who'd lived "the good life," but eternity would be much longer, their destiny sealed. He then realized how much better it is to live near to God. Perhaps hard times will come — actually they very likely will come. But God is good, all the time, both now and forever.

Even the hurts can be for the good. Steve would say it this way: "God never wastes a hurt." Steve knows that — not only through the unexpected death of his daughter but also through a life lived in the shadow of his own father's death. One of the most touching times where Steve told the story of how his father died was at a funeral. But it wasn't at Stephanie's services; it was at the funeral of Roni and Charity Bowers, the wife and daughter of Jim Bowers, who died when their plane was shot down over the Amazon River.

Steve was at the funeral in Michigan, not just to attend, but to speak because he knew something of loss. He knew the loss of a parent dying by a river in South America. His dad had been a missionary pilot and in 1956, his father, Nate Saint, along with Jim Elliot, Pete Fleming, Ed McCully, and Roger Youderian, died at the hands of Auca Indians.

Steve Saint was deeply moved at the funeral for Roni and Charity. When it was his time to share, he asked that he be excused because he really wanted to speak to the one person in the audience with whom he could identify the most: Cory, Jim and Roni Bowers' young son.

"A long time ago when I was just about your size, I was in a meeting just like this. I was sitting down there, and I really didn't know completely what was going on. . . . And you know, I was trying to figure out what was going on. We'd just had Christmas, and here all these people were coming back to our house, and I thought, 'Maybe we're going to have Christmas again.' A lot of people were crying and some people seemed to be sad. But in the midst of all that, other

people were laughing and I knew that something good was about to happen; I just didn't know what it was.

"You know, people have asked me about that, Cory, and I tell them that I didn't really understand what was going on. But now I understand it better. A lot of adults used a word then that I didn't understand. They used the word 'tragedy.' When tragic things happen, adults do really interesting things. They cry and sometimes they can be happy and sad at the same time. And these people were saying that what had happened before we came to that church service was something tragic. Now I'm kind of an old guy, and now when people come to me and they say, 'Oh I remember when that tragedy happened so long ago.' I know, Cory, that they were wrong.

"You see, my dad, who was a pilot like the man you probably call Uncle Kevin, and four of his really good friends had just been buried out in the jungles, and my mom told me that my dad was never coming home again. My mom wasn't really sad. So I asked her, 'Where did my dad go?' and she said, 'He went to live with Jesus.' And you know, that's where my mom and dad told me that we all wanted to go and live. Well, I thought, isn't that great that Daddy got to go sooner than the rest of us? And you know what? Now when people say, 'That was a tragedy,' I know they were wrong."[1]

The Needed Perspective

Do you see the perspective? It's not on the here-and-now, but on eternity. The word *tragedy* doesn't work! In a wonderful way, a man who knew exactly what it was like to sit where Cory was sitting that day made the truth simple for a young boy. The "grown-ups" who eavesdropped on the man's words to the boy heard the difference between people who don't know the Lord and those who do. The difference isn't that those who don't know Jesus have a life that's all pain and no joy — that just isn't so. The difference is this: "For them, the pain is fundamental and the joy is superficial because it won't last. For people who know the Lord, the pain is superficial and the joy is fundamental."[2]

Yes, Steve knows pain. He experienced the hurt of his father's death at the hands of Auca tribesmen and the hurt of his daughter's death. He also knows that God never wastes a hurt. In God's providence that day in Florida, as Steve stood by the hospital bed of Stephanie, alongside him were two special friends, Tementa and Mincaye, both elders from the Huaorani tribe, both Aucas. Mincaye was one of the men who'd killed Steve's father, Stephanie's grandfather. This is an amazing twist to the story, some would say. Others would see the hand of God at work, for the God who could reconcile sinful man with Himself could easily reconcile a man with one of those responsible for his father's death.

God really is good, isn't He? He uses different people in different situations to teach us that. From His Word we can learn the truth of His goodness, a truth that can be hidden from our hearts if we look only with our eyes. It's a truth that comes only when we look through eyes of faith. We see it fleshed out by Paul and Silas, who worshiped when it hurt, and by Habakkuk, who took his complaints to God and had his perspective change.

Perspective. A key word, an important concept. Asaph struggled until he put things into an eternal perspective, considering what would be the outcome of the lifestyles that had so shaken his steps. Actually, Habakkuk had struggled as well. He looked, saw the mess in Israel, cried out to God, and couldn't believe that God would use the Babylonians to do His work. But in the end Habakkuk also demonstrated the faith he talked about. He was determined to praise God not just "because of" but even "in spite of."

The Need to Put It into Practice

What's good for these people from Scripture is good for us as well. A day will come when few people will know the answer/response of "God is good. All the time." But the truth of this phrase will remain. It was true before someone came up with that answer/response, it's true now, and it will always be true because God truly is good all the time.

Will you make that truth the bedrock of your life?

"God is good," the man at the front said. The prisoners answered back, "All the time." "All the time," he said and they affirmed, "God is good." But there's more. What followed next were strong words of exhortation. I heard them often in that prison church: "You better know it, you better show it."

You can't just give lip service to the truth that "God is good." You must give life service, knowing, showing, putting it into practice.

The way to do that isn't by learning to say "All the time," when someone says, "God is good." The way is by learning and living the truths of the Word of God. Real people with real stories help us see these truths today. They're parents, business owners, Christian workers—flesh-and-blood people like your neighbors and the people at your church. They're not super-saints, but real people. They struggle with the deaths of their children, depression, seemingly senseless loss of life. Theirs are just a few stories in a world where the number of such testimonies is beyond imagination. In the midst of difficult times, they have experienced the truth that God is good. It upholds them, strengthens them, and guides them so that their feet don't slip, their steps don't falter.

You've learned eight vital truths that provide what you need to break out of the things that confine your soul. They're not eight steps to take in sequence; they're truths that swarm and surround. Embrace them all and find the reality of the goodness of God. Here they are:

1. *Sing.* Paul and Silas worshiped when it hurt. You must always aim your heart toward God, Who is always good.
2. *Have faith.* Things didn't look good in Habakkuk's day, and they might not look good in yours. But the righteous live by faith.
3. *Remember.* A temple musician hung up his harp, but then

determined to remember. When the difficult times come, remember — especially the goodness of God.

4. *Pray.* David may have been the king with all the trappings of royalty. But before his palace experience, he was hiding in caves and fleeing for his life. He prayed and so must you.

5. *Trust.* Jeremiah wasn't trying to write a hymn when he said, "Great is your faithfulness." He was stating a truth that encourages you to trust God in the trying times. Trust is a choice, one you must make when life seems to be anything but good and God seems to be unaware of what's happening.

6. *Live by the long view.* Romans 8:28 is a great verse, but it's just a slice of a tremendous section of Scripture. The major lesson of this passage is that when we live by the long view, we can know that God helps us in the hard times.

7. *Wait.* In a microwave, fast-food culture, waiting isn't natural. It's supernatural. Sometimes God tells you to wait, just as Joseph waited all those years in Egypt.

8. *Put it in practice.* You listen and learn the lessons. But then comes the day, the time when you must live them.

That God is good is a truth for today. It's a truth for you. No one can sprinkle pixie dust over your head so that from now on you walk along singing about God's goodness. No one can promise you that once you admit to this truth you'll never experience pain or discomfort. But this truth is better than that. This truth will carry you through the most challenging times of the days you draw breath on this earth, because you see beyond now, you see to then — eternity.

Life is hard, but it's short. Eternity is certain, and it's forever. So keep your eyes focused on the hope of heaven. Determine to live out the truth that God is good. Stay close to Jesus.

And perhaps one more time you need to get out your index card, or make room for more lipstick on the mirror. This time, two verses to learn:

*Surely God is good to Israel, to those who are
pure in heart. (Psalm 73:1)
But as for me, it is good to be near God. I have made the
Sovereign LORD my refuge; I will tell of all your deeds.
(verse 28)*

Study Guide

Part 1 — Getting into the Word
Prayer: As you begin this final study, do so as you began all the others, with prayer. Ask God to speak to you through His Word. Then be prepared to put into practice what you learn from Him and His Word. It's one thing to know what to do; it's another to do what God wants. Pray that He'll give you a greater desire to be obedient.

Reading and Hearing God's Word: Read Psalm 73, staying alert for verses or ideas that are especially relevant to your life. The psalmist isn't writing to entertain, but to instruct. Listen to learn so you can live the truths of this passage.

Understanding God's Word: Reread the psalm. This exercise isn't redundant, but intended to increase your grasp of the text. Now answer the following questions:

1. The psalmist said that his feet almost slipped. What caused his near fall?
2. Make a list of the characteristics of the wicked that are found in verses 4-12.
3. What was Asaph's conclusion in verse 13 when he compared his life with the life of the ungodly?
4. What changed his mind (see verse 17)?

Meditating on God's Word: Write a brief summary of a meaningful verse or idea from Psalm 73. Perhaps you have a desire to worship God in a way similar to the psalmist, recognizing that sometimes God teaches us in worship.

Part 2 — Taking the Word into My World

Redo the questions in the "Understanding God's Word" section, but make them personally relevant to you.

1. Does the prosperity of others affect you spiritually?
2. Can you make a list of characteristics of people today that's similar to Asaph's list?
3. Go over the psalmist's conclusion in verse 17 and compare it with your own attitude.
4. In a time of worship, ask God to help you put in practice His truths.

Part 3 — Grabbing Hold

Now's the time to get very specific. You've learned eight vital truths to help you break out of the things that imprison you, to find faith in faithless times, to know the reality of the truth that God is good.

1. First, list them again. Doing so will help you learn them!
2. Now evaluate which ones you do well with and which you need to improve. If you don't work at putting them into practice, you probably won't change. Resolve to live what you've learned.

EPILOGUE

The anticipated events for the first quarter of the New Year were basically three: I was scheduled to record radio messages for half of the Back to the Bible broadcasts, travel to speak at a variety of churches and conferences, and complete the final edit of my next book, *God Is Good*. Those three months looked great—on a calendar anyway.

Joshua became the theme of the radio broadcasts. I would tell people that I had "fallen in love with Joshua." Through the early chapters of the book I developed the theme, "Important Truths for Taking the Next Step into Uncertain Territory." Little did I know how pertinent those lessons would become.

The travel schedule was especially sweet. It wasn't too heavy, and included some very special opportunities and time with friends. I was able to go back to the prison to speak. This book is dedicated, "To the men of the church behind the wall, S.C.I. Dallas" for two reasons. First, it was there that the phrase "God is good" so impacted my life. Second, because those men had prayed that it would be published. They pray. Perhaps you need to be there to understand the full implications of that two-word sentence. It was a thrill to show them the cover and read them the dedication page.

It has been said that anyone can write but only writers can rewrite. I must be a writer, because March 1 was my deadline for the rewrite of the book. The editor returned the marked-up manuscript along with insightful comments on structure. Working with NavPress was proving to be a joy. Then with two unexpected events, the book became more autobiographical than I ever could have imagined.

On Martin Luther King Day I told Joan that I was going to get a physical—no problems, feeling fine, doing the treadmill thing aggressively, just wanted to update my tests. I had known for about twenty years that I had mitral valve prolapse and that it needed to be checked occasionally.

The next day, after recording three more messages of the next five-part series from Joshua, Wood Kroll called me to his office and told me that I was done. I knew finances at Back to the Bible had been heavily impacted by the financial downturn and that income had been poor, but did not expect the sudden end of my position. Initially, there was even a question as to whether I should finish recording the last two parts of that series. Suddenly, I was unemployed.

So I began to focus on three things: finding that next place of ministry, doing things that would produce income in the meantime such as speaking and writing, and getting my physical. Praying was automatic.

So we moved to the next round: the physical. First phase went well: cholesterol levels down, blood pressure down, even my weight down. Okay, two pounds, but hey, it was *down,* and for a skinny guy that was something. The job loss added some pressure—I needed to get the heart tests done before the hospitalization coverage ended. My severance package included only one more month of coverage.

The stress test went super and the echocardiogram showed the problem with the mitral valve—but it had worsened. No longer did I have a prolapse. I had regurgitation. The valve no longer closed but instead allowed a backwash in my heart. Some of my blood was moving the wrong direction. Rated on a scale of 0 to 4, mine was scored, prior to surgery, as a 5. After surgery, the doctor said that when he actually opened my heart, it was "worse than a 5."

Now a new race began. I had investigated less expensive hospitalization plans during the time I would be self-insured but had to cancel those. With surgery, I needed the better coverage, so COBRA was necessary. Plus the coverage was changing with the policy renewal on April 1 and I wanted to get as much done before that date as possible. And just to keep things interesting, I needed to finish the book, wanted to keep up my last few ministry opportunities for the first quarter, and we were trying to find that next place of ministry.

My wife, Joan, said at one point, "You can't schedule heart surgery the way you make a hair appointment," but we did.

God answered multiple prayers. I finished my speaking times in Florida and Nebraska, sent in the rewrite of the book, had significant interviews with prospective ministries, and then experienced the grace of God through open-heart surgery.

On Monday, March 25, 2002, I was in a catheterization lab watching my heart on a monitor. By Friday afternoon, I was at home—and for probably the first time in my entire life, I have no heart murmur and no hole in my heart.

We believe that it was of God's good grace that I was able to connect with one of the finest cardiovascular surgeons—right here in Lincoln, Nebraska. Dr. Deepak Gangahar was able to repair my mitral valve. While my heart was opened, he found the hole and repaired it as well. Prognosis is for a normal life. I will have periodic checkups and take a baby aspirin a day for the rest of my life.

Earlier I inwardly grumbled at the gap in my schedule for the second quarter. Evidently God had already penciled in "recovery."

The lessons are myriad. Top of the list is prayer. God has responded to the outpouring before His throne. Closely following are the lessons of His peace and provision. We know that He will continue to provide for our needs during this time. The truths from the Word of God taught in this book swarmed around me, some closer than others at times, but all there to help in time of great need. More than ever I realized that God did not give us steps to follow but assurances to grasp.

Cardiac surgery patients all have their pillows. It is given to you immediately following surgery so it can be held tightly against the sternum when you cough, to help minimize the pain. These truths of God need to be grasped in a similar way, held onto tightly—not just against the chest, but in the depth of our souls. And never forget that God is good. All the time.

Tony

NOTES

Chapter 2

1. J. David Hoke, "Making a Difference," 21 September 1997, www.horizonsnet.org/sermons/acts16.html.
2. "Reflections," *Christianity Today*, 3 September 2001, p. 98.
3. Ajith Fernando, *The NIV Application Commentary: Acts* (Grand Rapids, Mich.: Zondervan, 1998), p. 449.
4. Joseph Bayly, as quoted by R. Kent Hughes in *Acts* (Wheaton, Ill.: Crossway, 1996), p. 56.

Chapter 3

1. From the *Disciples' Study Bible* (Nashville, Tenn.: Holman Bible Publishers, 1988), p. 1127.

Chapter 4

1. Joel Lindsey and Pam Thum, "Life Is Hard (God is Good)," © 1995 Paragon Music (ASCAP) (Admin. By Brent–Benson Music Publishing, Inc.) / Designer Music / Songs of Lehsem (SESAC) All Rights Reserved. Used by permission.
2. Lindsey, Thum.
3. Lindsey, Thum.
4. James Montgomery Boice, *Psalms: An Expositional Commentary* (Grand Rapids, Mich.: Baker, 1998), p. 1189.
5. Lindsey, Thum.

Chapter 6

1. www.tanbible.com/tol_sng/greatisthyfaithfulness.htm.
2. From *The MacArthur Study Bible* (Nashville, Tenn.: Word, 1997), p. 1140.
3. Warren Wiersbe, *Expository Outlines of the Old Testament* (Covington, Ky.: Calvary Book Room, 1984), p. 278.

Chapter 7

1. http://stacks.msnbc.com/news/566085.asp.
2. R. Kent Hughes, *Romans* (Wheaton, Ill.: Crossway, 1991), p. 157.
3. C. S. Lewis, as quoted by Hughes, p. 159.
4. Hughes, pp. 162-163.
5. James Montgomery Boice, *Romans, Volume 2* (Grand Rapids, Mich.: Baker, 1997), p. 906.
6. http://www.backtothebible.org/radio/today/21369.

Chapter 8

1. Andrea Dufour, "God's Perfect Plan," *Cedarville Torch* 23, no. 3 (Fall 2001), p. 4.
2. From "Thought for Today" by E. C. Haskell, 25 October 2000, a daily e-mail note. Dr. Wheeler is a missionary serving in the Ukraine with the Association of Baptists for World Evangelism.
3. "Reflections," *Christianity Today*, 4 September 2000, p. 112.
4. Dufour.

Chapter 9

1. Steve Saint, "God Never Wastes a Hurt," www.abwe.org/family/peru_incident/memorials/service_michigan.htm.
2. Ibid.

AUTHOR

TONY BECKETT received his M.Div. from Biblical Theological Seminary of Hatfield, Pennsylvania, and his D.Min. from Trinity Evangelical Divinity School of Deerfield, Illinois. He has more than twenty years of pastoral experience serving churches in Iowa, Ohio, and Pennsylvania, as well as working with mission agencies, camps, and church leadership councils. His ministry also includes having served as an associate Bible teacher for Back to the Bible, an international ministry in Lincoln, Nebraska.

In his spare time, you can find him enjoying a baseball game and a bag of peanuts with his wife, Joan, their three daughters, Katie, Bekah, and Lauren, and Bekah's husband, Mark.